SpringerBriefs in Political Science

SpringerBriefs present concise summaries of cutting-edge research and practical applications across a wide spectrum of fields. Featuring compact volumes of 50 to 125 pages, the series covers a range of content from professional to academic. Typical topics might include:

- A timely report of state-of-the art analytical techniques
- A bridge between new research results, as published in journal articles, and a contextual literature review
- A snapshot of a hot or emerging topic
- An in-depth case study or clinical example
- A presentation of core concepts that students must understand in order to make independent contributions

SpringerBriefs in Political Science showcase emerging theory, empirical research, and practical application in political science, policy studies, political economy, public administration, political philosophy, international relations, and related fields, from a global author community.

SpringerBriefs are characterized by fast, global electronic dissemination, standard publishing contracts, standardized manuscript preparation and formatting guidelines, and expedited production schedules.

Sergei Golunov · Assel Bitabar

Bridging Borders

Central Asian Cross-Border Cooperation
in a Comparative Global Perspective

 Springer

Sergei Golunov
Suleyman Demirel University
Kaskelen, Kazakhstan

Assel Bitabar
KAZGUU University
Astana, Kazakhstan

ISSN 2191-5466   ISSN 2191-5474 (electronic)
SpringerBriefs in Political Science
ISBN 978-3-031-84252-8   ISBN 978-3-031-84253-5 (eBook)
https://doi.org/10.1007/978-3-031-84253-5

© The Author(s) 2025. This book is an open access publication.

Open Access This book is licensed under the terms of the Creative Commons Attribution 4.0 International License (http://creativecommons.org/licenses/by/4.0/), which permits use, sharing, adaptation, distribution and reproduction in any medium or format, as long as you give appropriate credit to the original author(s) and the source, provide a link to the Creative Commons license and indicate if changes were made.

The images or other third party material in this book are included in the book's Creative Commons license, unless indicated otherwise in a credit line to the material. If material is not included in the book's Creative Commons license and your intended use is not permitted by statutory regulation or exceeds the permitted use, you will need to obtain permission directly from the copyright holder.

The use of general descriptive names, registered names, trademarks, service marks, etc. in this publication does not imply, even in the absence of a specific statement, that such names are exempt from the relevant protective laws and regulations and therefore free for general use.

The publisher, the authors and the editors are safe to assume that the advice and information in this book are believed to be true and accurate at the date of publication. Neither the publisher nor the authors or the editors give a warranty, expressed or implied, with respect to the material contained herein or for any errors or omissions that may have been made. The publisher remains neutral with regard to jurisdictional claims in published maps and institutional affiliations.

This Springer imprint is published by the registered company Springer Nature Switzerland AG
The registered company address is: Gewerbestrasse 11, 6330 Cham, Switzerland

If disposing of this product, please recycle the paper.

Acknowledgments

This research is supported by the Science Committee of the Ministry of Science and Higher Education of the Republic of Kazakhstan (grant no. AP23489647, "Cross-Border Cooperation of Kazakhstan with Neighboring Central Asian Countries").

This study utilized artificial intelligence assistance (ChatGPT) for translation and technical text editing.

All maps included in the work were generated using the Mapchart service (mapchart.net).

Contents

1 Introduction 1
2 Overview of Global Cross-Border Cooperation Experience 7
3 Central Asian Cross-Border Cooperation 71
4 Adapting Global Cross-Border Cooperation Experiences
  for Central Asia 107

Conclusion 115
Bibliography 119

Chapter 1
Introduction

1.1 Introduction

Cross-border cooperation (CBC), as cooperation between actors in neighboring territories aimed at achieving constructive and locally beneficial goals, represents a crucial—and often indispensable—condition for the successful development of border areas. Without CBC these areas would often remain in a marginal logistical position with a reduced range of connections and partnerships with neighboring territories. The development of cross-border ties, however, offers an opportunity for dynamic growth by combining the potentials of adjacent regions and leveraging their differences as a stimulus for revitalizing cross-border trade, mobility, investments, and other flows. Moreover, intensive cross-border cooperation can serve as a platform for cultural enrichment, knowledge sharing, and improving relations between communities in neighboring countries.

This study focuses on CBC in Central Asia—a region comprising Kazakhstan, Kyrgyzstan, Tajikistan, Turkmenistan, and Uzbekistan. It excludes the land borders of these countries with extra-regional neighbors—Afghanistan, Iran, China, and Russia—even though, from the perspective of Central Asian states themselves, the Kazakhstan–Russia border, as well as the borders of Kazakhstan, Kyrgyzstan, and Tajikistan with China, are generally of greater economic importance compared to their borders with other neighbors within the region. It is not surprising as the economies of Central Asian states remain heavily reliant on extra-regional actors rather than being oriented toward intraregional cooperation. When discussing CBC in a given region, it is essential to acknowledge that such cooperation has been occurring within the context of relatively limited regional cohesion.

Nevertheless, the internal interstate borders of post-Soviet Central Asia can be seen as an underutilized resource, activation of which could provide a significant boost to socio-economic development and strengthen cooperative relationships between local communities. CBC among Central Asian countries has the potential to mitigate the landlocked position of the region, particularly that of Uzbekistan, which

© The Author(s) 2025
S. Golunov and A. Bitabar, *Bridging Borders*,
SpringerBriefs in Political Science, https://doi.org/10.1007/978-3-031-84253-5_1

is double-landlocked and lacks borders with either China or Russia. By softening the barrier effect of borders and fostering the development of efficient cross-border transport corridors within the region, CBC can create opportunities for improved connectivity. Moreover, CBC could play a pivotal role in advancing the nascent Central Asian integration process, helping to blur political and cultural divides while connecting adjacent territories.

The effectiveness of CBC in Central Asia can potentially be enhanced through the systematic and impactful application of experiences from other countries and regions. To date, a substantial body of CBC-related experience has been accumulated outside Central Asia. Particularly noteworthy is the experience of the European Union, where CBC has been integrated into broader agendas of regional development and integration. Other countries and regions, such as North America, China, Southeast Asia, and Latin America, have also achieved significant and commendable results in this field. As this study will demonstrate, applying these experiences in Central Asia will likely require adapting the specific components of CBC strategies and practices to local conditions, including selecting those most suitable for these conditions and discarding or significantly modifying others.

The purpose of this study is to conceptualize the international experience of CBC on a global scale and analyze its applicability to CBC among the post-Soviet Central Asian countries. What are the achievements and shortcomings of the experiences of the selected countries and regions? Which specific CBC strategies from these countries and regions can be highlighted? What is the nature of the unique conditions shaping CBC in Central Asia? To what extent, and in what ways, can the aforementioned strategies from external countries and regions be adapted to the conditions of Central Asia?

Answering these questions requires meticulous research and the processing of diverse information from various regions of the world. To date, both conceptual and empirical studies on CBC published in reputable, high-ranking journals exhibit a clear bias toward examining the experience of the European Union. A smaller, though more significant, body of work focuses on the North American region, particularly on U.S.–Canada and U.S.–Mexico CBC. In contrast, studies on CBC in other regions are markedly less prominent in the academic literature.

Comparative studies on CBC across different regions are particularly scarce. Most comparative analyses have concentrated on contrasting the experiences of the EU and North America (Scott 1999; Blatter and Clement 2000; Koff 2015; Longo 2016; Herzog and Sohn 2019; Peña and Durand 2022). A small number of studies focus on comparisons involving other regional pairs, such as the EU and Southeast Asia (Nadalutti and Rüland 2024), the EU and China (Kosonen et al. 2008), or the EU and Africa (Aluede 2023). An attempt at providing a global overview of CBC experiences was made by (Brunet-Jailly 2022); however, the analysis proved to be brief and fragmented.

While the topic of Central Asian borders attracts significant academic interest, most studies prioritize either intraregional territorial disputes or CBC along the region's external borders with China and Russia. Comprehensive studies on CBC within the internal borders of the Central Asian region are extremely rare. The

1.1 Introduction

closest attempt to such an analysis was made in a report by the Asian Development Bank (Asian Development Bank 2020), which examined CBC challenges in selected regions of the member states of the Central Asia Regional Economic Cooperation Program (CAREC), including the Fergana Valley. Although the report's analysis of the global CBC experience was extremely brief and superficial, it provided an in-depth examination of local CBC agendas and generated numerous recommendations based on this analysis. These recommendations hold significant value for conceptualizing the regional CBC agenda and for formulating further policy suggestions rooted in this conceptualization. A number of studies focus on specific aspects of CBC in the region, including the issue of informal trade and border markets (Kaminski and Mitra 2012), borderland demographic trends (Polat 2002), as well as transboundary water management (Mukhammadiev 2014). Additionally, a substantial number of shorter studies published in local journals address specific and localized aspects of CBC within the region.

Considering the existing body of scholarship, this work is likely the first detailed study that aims both to provide a comprehensive conceptualization of CBC on a global scale and to conceptualize CBC between the countries of post-Soviet Central Asia. Additionally, it seeks to offer a conceptual analysis of the applicability of international CBC practices to the Central Asian context.

This study has several significant limitations. First, while the analysis of CBC in each of the examined regions, including Central Asia, offers a starting point for understanding the topic, a more structured and detailed examination would require further, region-specific studies. Second, the focus is primarily on CBC strategies, with considerably less attention paid to specific techniques and practices, which were central to the recommendation part of the aforementioned Asian Development Bank report. Third, the research is based on comparative qualitative policy analysis and does not incorporate quantitative statistical or sociological studies, which could have offered more nuanced insights into the issue. Finally, some regions, such as South Asia and the Middle East, were excluded from the scope of this study, and the analysis of Africa does not fully reflect the subregional specificities of its various areas.

The structure of this monograph is organized as follows. The *Introduction* (co-authored by S. Golunov and A. Bitabar) outlines the research problems, objectives, niche, limitations, and structure of the study.

The *First Chapter*, authored by Sergei Golunov, analyzes CBC experiences in selected regions and countries. It includes chapters dedicated to CBC in the EU, North America, China (this section is co-authored by S. Golunov and A. Bitabar), Southeast Asia, Latin America, Africa, and Russia.

The *Second Chapter,* mostly co-authored by Sergei Golunov and Assel Bitabar, addresses the specifics of CBC in Central Asia. It features chapters on the conceptual issues of CBC in the region as a whole, as well as CBC in individual Central Asian states: Uzbekistan (authored by A. Bitabar), Kazakhstan (authored by S. Golunov), Turkmenistan, Kyrgyzstan, and Tajikistan.

The *Third Chapter,* authored by S. Golunov, examines the opportunities and limitations of applying international CBC practices to the Central Asian context.

Finally, the co-authored *Conclusion* synthesizes the key findings of the study.

The authors express their deep gratitude to the OSCE Academy in Bishkek for supporting this monograph project following the results of a competitive selection process. We are also thankful to the Ministry of Science and Higher Education of Kazakhstan, whose financial support for the project "Kazakhstan's Cross-Border Cooperation with Central Asian Countries" significantly expanded our access to resources and tools that enhanced the collection and analysis of information during the preparation of this book. We also extend our gratitude to our assistant Assyl Duisen for aiding in the collection of relevant information.

The authors hope that this work will inspire further research on the comparative study of CBC, the conceptualization of CBC in Central Asia, and the potential application of international experience to the development of CBC frameworks both in Central Asia and in other regions of the world. It is also hoped that this study will prove useful for policymakers in Central Asia and beyond, providing a basis for the development of region-specific strategic CBC concepts.

References

Aluede, Jackson A. 2023. A review of cross-border cooperation in Europe and Africa since the second half of the twentieth century. *Nigerian Journal of Humanities* 28: 142–166.

Asian Development Bank. 2020. *Strengthening cross-border community collaboration in the CAREC region: A scoping study*, 0 ed. Manila, Philippines: Asian Development Bank. https://doi.org/10.22617/TCS200414-2.

Blatter, Joachim, and Norris Clement. 2000. II introduction to the volume: Cross-border cooperation in Europe: Historical development, institutionalization, and contrasts with North America. *Journal of Borderlands Studies* 15 (1): 14–53. https://doi.org/10.1080/08865655.2000.9695541.

Brunet-Jailly, Emmanuel. 2022. Cross-border cooperation: A global overview. *Alternatives: Global, Local, Political* 47 (1): 3–17. https://doi.org/10.1177/03043754211073463.

Herzog, Lawrence A., and Christophe Sohn. 2019. The co-mingling of bordering dynamics in the San Diego-Tijuana cross-border metropolis. *Territory, Politics, Governance* 7 (2): 177–199. https://doi.org/10.1080/21622671.2017.1323003.

Kaminski, Bartlomiej, and Saumya Mitra. 2012. *Borderless bazaars and regional integration in Central Asia: Emerging patterns of trade and cross-border cooperation*. Washington, DC: The World Bank.

Koff, Harlan. 2015. Informal economies in European and American cross-border regions. *Journal of Borderlands Studies* 30 (4): 469–487. https://doi.org/10.1080/08865655.2016.1165133.

Kosonen, Riitta, Xu Feng, and Erja Kettunen. 2008. Paired border towns or TwinCities from Finland and China. *Chinese Journal of Population Resources and Environment* 6 (1): 3–13. https://doi.org/10.1080/10042857.2008.10684849.

Longo, Matthew. 2016. A '21st century border'? Cooperative border controls in the US and EU after 9/11. *Journal of Borderlands Studies* 31 (2): 187–202.

Mukhammadiev, Bakhtiyor. 2014. Challenges of transboundary water resources management in Central Asia. In *The Aral Sea: The Devastation and partial rehabilitation of a Great Lake*, ed. Philip Micklin, N.V. Aladin, and Igor Plotnikov, 233–251. Berlin, Heidelberg: Springer. https://doi.org/10.1007/978-3-642-02356-9_9.

Nadalutti, Elisabetta, and Jürgen Rüland. 2024. Cross-border regionalism in the EU and ASEAN: Another dimension of the 'Varieties of Regionalism.' *Journal of European Integration* March: 1–22. https://doi.org/10.1080/07036337.2024.2329636.

References

Peña, Sergio, and Frédéric. Durand. 2022. Mobility planning in cross-border metropolitan regions: The European and North American experiences. *Territory, Politics, Governance* 10 (2): 219–236. https://doi.org/10.1080/21622671.2020.1769716.

Polat, Necati. 2002. *Boundary Issues in Central Asia*. Ardsley, NY: Transnational Publishers.

Scott, James Wesley. 1999. European and North American contexts for cross-border regionalism. *Regional Studies* 33 (7): 605–617. https://doi.org/10.1080/00343409950078657.

Open Access This chapter is licensed under the terms of the Creative Commons Attribution 4.0 International License (http://creativecommons.org/licenses/by/4.0/), which permits use, sharing, adaptation, distribution and reproduction in any medium or format, as long as you give appropriate credit to the original author(s) and the source, provide a link to the Creative Commons license and indicate if changes were made.

The images or other third party material in this chapter are included in the chapter's Creative Commons license, unless indicated otherwise in a credit line to the material. If material is not included in the chapter's Creative Commons license and your intended use is not permitted by statutory regulation or exceeds the permitted use, you will need to obtain permission directly from the copyright holder.

Chapter 2
Overview of Global Cross-Border Cooperation Experience

2.1 Conceptual Dimension of Cross-Border Cooperation

The topic of CBC has been extensively studied in numerous works. These studies address the conceptualization of various aspects of this phenomenon, evaluate its effectiveness, and propose recommendations for its improvement and for overcoming the numerous challenges it faces.

Most definitions of CBC are based on the official definition provided by the Madrid Convention of 1980, which emphasizes strengthening good-neighborly relations between local authorities or communities in adjacent territories (Council of Europe 1980). This definition, however, complicates the inclusion of spontaneous forms of CBC deeply embedded in the local border social order. Such forms, inspired by Rumford's concept of "vernacular borderwork" (the daily practices of creating and reinforcing borders by ordinary people), can be described as "vernacular" CBC (Rumford 2014). These may include activities such as cross-border shuttle trade. Moreover, one could raise the conceptual question of whether illegal cross-border activities should be considered a form of CBC. The Madrid Convention definition also assumes a favorable political climate and, typically, the officially expressed willingness of both sides to develop such cooperation. However, in some cases, CBC can emerge through the efforts of enthusiasts or professionals despite an unfavorable political climate and the reluctance of neighboring states to intensify cross-border ties (Arieli 2016; Golunov 2021).

CBC can take a wide variety of forms. It may develop through ceremonial official events and formal cultural exchanges, the establishment of joint governance bodies for cross-border projects and systematic collaborative planning, initiatives by non-governmental organizations, or adopting the concept of vernacular cross-border cooperation, profit-driven stable individual cross-border connections.

Evaluating the effectiveness of CBC is challenging due to the differing starting conditions faced by cooperating actors in various cases, as well as the broad range of functions that CBC performs—many of which are not easily measurable in quantitative terms. Starting conditions, in particular, may be shaped by unfavorable factors such as poor interstate relations; strict border controls; insufficient authority of local governments involved in cooperation; lack of information on cross-border opportunities; the absence of a widely used lingua franca or significant cultural differences in border regions; weak infrastructure; limited financial support; or extreme economic disparities—whether too small or too large—between neighboring sides, both of which can reduce their mutual economic attractiveness (Blatter and Clement 2000). The wide range of functions that CBC can perform includes, for example, reducing the rigidity of both tangible and intangible border-related barriers (e.g., legal and cultural), overcoming the marginalization of border areas, creating jobs, implementing commercial projects, developing sustainable cross-border networks, engaging in joint cross-border infrastructure planning, mitigating ethnic and political conflicts, increasing mutual awareness between neighboring sides, and more (Sousa 2013).

Based on the functional purposes of cross-border cooperation, as well as its intensity, duration, and stability, De Sousa identifies three types of CBC: awareness-raising (e.g., official visits), mutual aid (sporadic assistance, such as in emergencies), and functional (long-term projects aimed at creating permanent cross-border mechanisms, for instance in transport or tourism) (Sousa 2013). It is also important not to overlook the dimension of using the border as a resource. In this context, either the rigidity of border barriers or their relaxation creates economic and other opportunities for borderland actors. A border region's location can either make it logistically attractive to external investors or provide border communities with opportunities for mutually beneficial knowledge and experience exchange (Sohn 2014).

Amid the wide variety of factors that can either stimulate or hinder the development of CBC, we would like to emphasize the following aspects.

One of the key factors, encompassing both physical and intangible dimensions, is the proximity between adjacent territories and the participants in CBC. Proximity does not necessarily equate to physical distance (physical proximity), which does not inherently guarantee quick and effective physical or virtual communication between cooperation participants. Unfavorable landscapes (natural barriers), the lack of fast and convenient transport links (transport proximity), and border delays can significantly increase the time required for physical connections between neighboring territories. The so-called "death of distance" due to the diffusion of information and communication technologies (Cairncross 1997), proclaimed by some researchers, appears to have been somewhat exaggerated, as distance and transport proximity still play a significant role not only in trade but even in the dissemination of information (Capello et al. 2018). Cultural proximity, including a shared language for communication and the degree of cultural similarity, as well as cognitive proximity and other forms of proximity (Lundquist and Trippl 2013), can also play a crucial role in fostering cross-border communication.

One of the key indicators of the success of CBC is often considered the sustainability and density of cross-border network connections among both formal and informal actors (Svensson and Nordlund 2015). The very fact of successfully maintaining such connections is frequently regarded as a significant achievement. Cross-border networks provide a foundation for stable cooperation, the initiation of new projects, and the active involvement of network members in joint efforts. Truly cross-border projects of this nature foster intensified interaction between neighboring territories. In contrast, the more common format, where each side implements its part of a joint project separately within its own territory, contributes much less to such intensification.

In turn, the successful organization of cross-border networks and projects largely depends on intangible factors such as trust, the will to implement projects, leadership, and the competence or effectiveness of the participating parties (Hataley and Leuprecht 2018). For instance, the role of trust is particularly significant in cases where the legal framework for CBC has significant gaps.

As some researchers rightly point out, dominant conceptualizations of CBC are Eurocentric (Scott 2017) or, considering that studies of North American CBC are the second most frequent, broadly Western-centric. Indeed, the evident majority of scholarly works on CBC focus on the European Union, which partially skews researchers' conceptual frameworks by shaping biased perceptions of what should be considered universal norms and what constitutes deviations in CBC. As will be demonstrated further, in several key respects—including the high success of the European integration project, democratic decision-making, extensive regional powers in CBC, and generous funding for cross-border projects—the EU's experience can be regarded as an anomaly rather than a norm on a global scale. A particularly striking aberration in the thematic priorities of CBC conceptualizations is the secondary attention that most mainstream studies devote to the challenges of securing funding for CBC projects—a problem that is significantly easier to address within the EU compared to other regions of the world. At the same time, the most common form of CBC that does not require substantial funding—namely, informal cross-border trade—is relatively frequently studied in the context of CBC in European and North American regions (Bruns and Miggelbrink 2012; Koff 2015). However, it is rarely analyzed as a distinct issue within the framework of CBC itself. Instead, it is often examined through other lenses, such as competition between shuttle traders and the state.

The Eurocentrism of current CBC conceptualizations also manifests in the pronounced emphasis on formalized CBC and insufficient attention to spontaneous, vernacular forms of collaboration. These and other issues require further exploration within the CBC research agenda to make it more universal and balanced.

2.2 European Union

The CBC model of the EU far surpasses other regional models in terms of effectiveness and sophistication. In no other part of the world does CBC receive such systematic official support, including integration into long-term policy frameworks and generous funding. Nor does it rely on such a well-developed legal foundation, institutional infrastructure, and a comprehensive system of recommendations refined over decades. The EU's CBC framework has implemented the largest number of successful projects across the broadest range of fields, including joint planning for border area development, transportation, manufacturing, trade, innovation, the development of cross-border labor markets, environmental protection, healthcare, education, tourism, culture, information sharing, emergency management, and much more.

The EU's experience of CBC developed within a unique historical context. Initially, its key drivers included the participants' desire to foster social reconciliation after World War II (Wassenberg 2017) and to achieve economic benefits from the reduction of border barriers in the context of emerging integration. Over time, CBC became more deeply integrated into the ideology and policy framework of European integration and began receiving systematic multibillion-euro financial support. This was further bolstered by the creation of the Eurozone, which eliminated financial costs associated with currency exchange operations (Fig. 2.1).

From an ideological perspective, CBC came to be seen as a tool for blurring borders and reconfiguring spaces shaped by nation-states through the creation of cross-border regions intended to serve as connective seams between border areas (Blatter and Clement 2000). Politically and economically, priorities shifted from fostering bilateral relations between neighboring regions and overcoming their

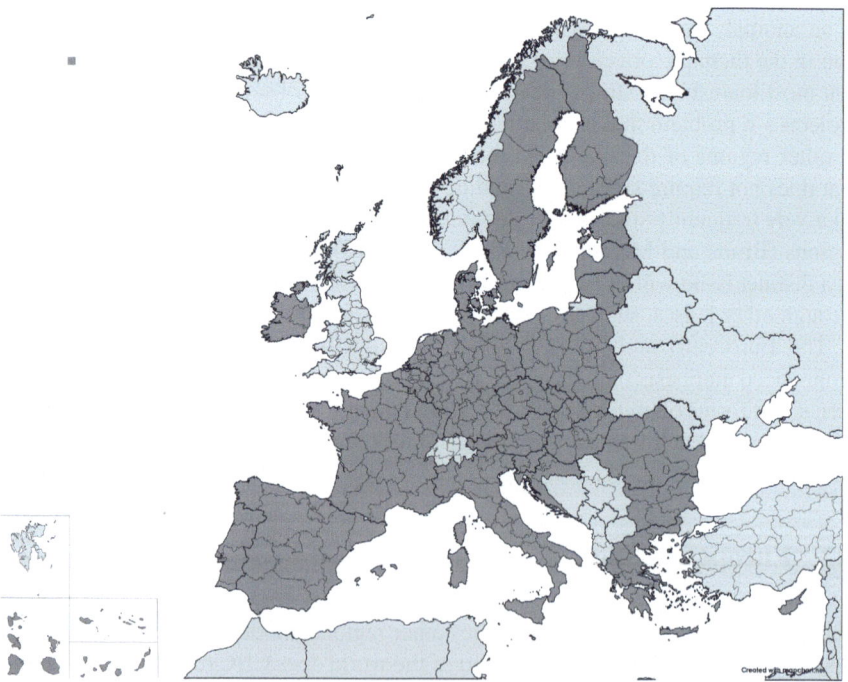

Fig. 2.1 European Union states with their administrative regions

2.2 European Union

marginal economic and geographic status to using CBC as a tool for cohesion policy, regional development (Frank 2013), and the integration of candidate countries into the EU. Additionally, CBC in the EU is rooted in liberal-democratic values and principles of decentralization and multilevel governance. It involves broad participation in decision-making processes by governmental and non-governmental actors across various levels and delegates decision-making to the lowest appropriate level.

All of this makes the EU's CBC model highly specific and difficult to fully replicate in other regions. Yet, at least some elements of the EU's CBC experience hold significant value for cross-border cooperation in any other part of the world.

The development of CBC in the EU has yielded numerous positive outcomes. According to some estimates, border opening within the EU has led to a 2.7% increase in regional gross value added (GVA) per capita, while doubling the number of CBC project partners per 100,000 population results in a 2.3% increase in regional GVA per capita (Basboga 2022). Among the many positive trends and effects observed as a result of this cooperation, the following can be highlighted:

- Overcoming the marginal economic status of many border regions (Fritsch et al. 2015) and their full integration into the European Single Market (Liberato et al. 2018);
- Mitigating economic development disparities between neighboring regions (Jakubowski et al. 2022);
- Developing and optimizing cross-border transport infrastructure (Christmann et al. 2020);
- A sharp increase in the number of cross-border regional organizations since the 1950s, now exceeding one hundred;
- Establishing a complementary system for providing services to populations on both sides of the border (e.g., in education, healthcare, and public utilities) (Basboga 2022);
- Preventing or slowing the depopulation of border areas (Cairo et al. 2024);
- The growing role of local and non-governmental actors in cooperation (Yndigegn 2013);
- Long-term growth in cross-border mobility (Klatt 2014);
- Creating new jobs and cross-border labor markets (Pires and Nunes 2018);
- Increasing the intensity of cross-border exchanges of economic, cultural, and other types of information (Church and Reid 1996).
- Establishment and development of cross-border network partnerships and increased mutual trust between partners (Meijerink 2014);
- In some cases, a shift in cooperation from isolated projects to systematic cross-border planning in infrastructure, socio-economic, and other areas (Fricke 2015);
- Improved efficiency in cross-border environmental protection efforts (Renner et al. 2018);
- Overcoming past conflicts (Wassenberg 2017) and partially dismantling stereotypes about neighboring sides (Spierings and Van Der Velde 2013);
- Stimulating and disseminating innovations born out of cross-border partnerships;

- Expanding cooperation to include broader territories beyond neighboring provinces, some of which do not directly border one another;
- Enhanced attractiveness of border areas for tourists (Więckowski 2023) and creating joint recreational facilities through collaboration (Kramsch 2001);
- Intensified cross-border cultural exchanges (Gubrium et al. 2024);
- Partial integration and optimization of governance systems in twin cities located in close proximity (Asher 2012).
- Increasing the capacity of the EU's external borders, fostering cooperation with non-EU partners in security and crime prevention, and facilitating border crossing for residents of border areas (Domaniewski and Studzińska 2016).

European CBC has spurred innovative uses of territories and their potential (Van Den Broek et al. 2020). Examples include the development of infrastructure (e.g., transport and industrial facilities) designed to serve multiple neighboring territories, thereby eliminating duplication (Sousa 2013), and the promotion of tourism in tripoint borderland areas, leveraging the uniqueness and multicultural nature of these regions to attract visitors (Więckowski 2023).

The evolution of CBC in the EU has led to the creation of numerous innovative solutions aimed at enhancing the effectiveness of implemented initiatives. Political democracy and consistent political support for CBC have provided a favorable environment for such innovations. Some authors emphasize that EU CBC, at its core, represents a process of experimentation with new forms of cooperation and governance (Sousa 2013), the generation and dissemination of new knowledge, and mutual learning of innovative practices (Faludi 2008).

Systematic competitive project funding has resulted in the development of guidelines, planning and monitoring systems, and methods and criteria for evaluating effectiveness. As the focus of grant support has gradually shifted, at least in part, from bilateral projects to multilateral ones involving broader (including non-border) regions, priorities and management methods have had to adapt to increasingly complex conditions.

An important aspect of some EU CBC projects is the development and promotion of cross-border identity (Gasparini 2014). This fosters cohesion among border region communities and helps overcome barriers created by nationalist perceptions and by those official policies that accentuate differences between neighboring territories. Practices for promoting cross-border identity may include joint events or branding of the cross-border region as a whole or specific sites within it. However, efforts to promote cross-border identity have met with mixed success, as nationalist sentiments and practices remain deeply entrenched (Calzada 2015).

The EU's CBC has an unparalleled institutional and legal framework in terms of its sophistication, comprising various elements. The most influential organizational mechanisms and legal norms of European CBC have been shaped primarily by two key contributors: active border regions on the one hand, and the highest governing bodies of the European Union on the other.

Historically, the first widely adopted organizational mechanisms for CBC were created by the border regions themselves. Starting in the late 1950s, Euroregions

2.2 European Union

began to emerge—cross-border territorial entities usually established by the authorities of two or more border regions. While some Euroregions have proven their effectiveness over time, establishing permanent joint governance bodies, including secretariats, joint accounts, and adopting numerous legal acts, the activities of others have been less significant, often limited to ceremonial functions (Perkmann 2007b). Even the most effective Euroregions have severely limited formal powers and, typically, function more as information hubs, organizers, and lobbyists for specific cooperation projects than as governance centers for systematic collaboration between border areas (Klatt and Herrmann 2011).

To coordinate the activities of EU border regions and represent their interests before the authorities of the European Economic Community (EEC), the Association of European Border Regions (AEBR) was established in 1971. As of today, it includes around 100 Euroregions. The AEBR has been relatively successful in advocating for the interests of border regions at the national and European levels and has played a significant role in integrating CBC into the EU's regional development policies.

One relatively recent example of AEBR's effectiveness is the B-solutions project, launched under its auspices in 2018. The project provides legal support on a competitive basis to CBC participants facing cross-border legal or administrative barriers. As of May 2024, the project has supported approximately 150 cases (Inforegio—B Solutions 2024). Another example is AEBR's successful lobbying efforts to address the needs of cross-border labor markets during the COVID-19 pandemic (Opioła and Böhm 2022). The AEBR's achievements influenced the creation of the European Committee of the Regions in 1994—a consultative EU body authorized to issue official opinions on legislation affecting regional development.

Since the 1980s, the highest bodies of the EEC/EU have become actively involved in establishing the institutional framework for European CBC. One of the first comprehensive tools for managing European cross-border cooperation was the 1980 European Outline Convention on Transfrontier Co-operation between Territorial Communities or Authorities (commonly known as the 1980 Madrid Convention). This convention defined CBC as any joint action aimed at fostering good-neighborly relations between territorial authorities or communities under the jurisdiction of two or more parties and created the legal framework for establishing cross-border regions (Council of Europe 1980). The 1995 Additional Protocol to the Convention clarified its provisions and introduced additional mechanisms for concluding CBC agreements in line with national legislation. Notably, it allowed for the creation of governing bodies for cross-border regions with legal personality, determined by the location of the governing body's headquarters (Council of Europe 1995).

European CBC gained new momentum with its inclusion in the framework of European regional policy (cohesion policy), which provided it with stable and long-term financial support. Established in 1975, the European Regional Development Fund (ERDF) began supporting the Interreg CBC programs in 1989. The Interreg programs are divided into three strands: Strand A supports cross-border cooperation, Strand B promotes transnational cooperation among large groups of regions (not necessarily adjacent), and Strand C focuses on forming interregional networks for information and experience sharing. Interreg programs fund both large-scale and smaller projects involving EU regions in CBC with internal and external partners. Starting from the third Interreg program, these initiatives have been structured in seven-year cycles. The budget for the sixth program, running from 2021 to 2027, amounts to approximately €10 billion (European Commission n.d.).

Since the 1990s, increasing emphasis has been placed on multilateral CBC projects involving broad territories across multiple countries. In other words, the focus has shifted towards the creation of mesoregions (e.g., the EUSALP region, encompassing territories from 48 regions across seven member states (EUSALP n.d.)). On the one hand, the spillover of CBC into new territories (including areas not directly adjacent to borders) and sectors can enhance the overall capacity of participants, potentially improving the effectiveness of cooperation. On the other hand, it can complicate the management of joint projects.

Interreg is currently the largest source of funding for CBC projects in the EU, with support from other sources being incomparable in scale to this initiative. It is widely acknowledged that Interreg has fundamentally transformed the nature of CBC in the EU, becoming the primary funding mechanism for projects and providing a strong incentive for many actors to actively participate. The program's success is particularly notable in areas such as job creation and infrastructure development (Cairo et al. 2024).

However, the Interreg format has also created a significant challenge for long-term planning. Many participants focus on obtaining relatively short-term funding without designing projects with a long-term perspective in mind (Shepherd and Ioannides 2020). Additionally, it should be noted that the total funding provided by Interreg—ranging from tens to several hundred million euros per seven-year period for individual cross-border regions—is still often insufficient to fully meet the needs of cross-border development (Sarmiento-Mirwaldt and Roman-Kamphaus 2013).

Despite significant efforts to support CBC, cross-border cooperation institutions often remained in a state of legal uncertainty between national jurisdictions. To address this issue, the EU introduced the legal mechanism of the European Grouping of Territorial Cooperation (EGTC) in 2006 (Regulation 1082/2006 2006), which facilitates the creation of legal entities for CBC under European law. This mechanism allows official authorities or non-governmental organizations from neighboring countries to open joint accounts and manage CBC activities more effectively. The powers of EGTCs are primarily limited to organizing and managing CBC projects and programs rather than systematically governing cross-border territories. Critics of this mechanism, however, point out that in some cases, its implementation leads to burdensome bureaucratization of CBC (Caesar 2017), increased control by official authorities, and the disharmonious overlap of EGTC regulations with national legal frameworks (Evrard 2016).

In 2004, the European Neighbourhood Policy (ENP) was launched as a cooperation instrument supported financially by the European Investment Bank. The ENP aims to develop cooperation between the EU and its neighboring countries and regions, facilitating EU accession for some neighboring states while fostering less binding good-neighborly relations with others. It should be noted that CBC is only one of several areas addressed by the ENP and not its primary focus, as reflected in

2.2 European Union

the allocation of funding. Still, the ENP marked a significant step forward compared to previous funding schemes, particularly by enabling a single application for joint projects (Khasson 2013).

The ENP has also faced criticism, with the main argument being that the EU has used it to systematically impose its priorities and interests on cooperation partners (Dimitrovova 2012). Critics have also pointed to the EU's excessive focus on security issues and the imbalance in CBC capacities between EU countries with more decentralized governance systems and their partners, where border regions often lack sufficient decision-making powers (Sousa 2013).

In 2018, the European Commission proposed the European Cross-Border Mechanism (ECBM) as a new tool to eliminate legal barriers to CBC. The proposal aimed to allow one participating party to voluntarily apply the legislation of a neighboring country for cross-border infrastructure or service projects. However, the concept of partial legal sovereignty concession, even on a voluntary basis, raised concerns among some EU member states, resulting in prolonged discussions and delays in advancing the mechanism (European Parliament 2018).

The legal frameworks established by the EU have also fostered CBC in specific sectors. For example, the foundation for cross-border cooperation in healthcare was laid by Directive 2011/24/EU, which addresses patients' rights in accessing cross-border healthcare services and defines reimbursement mechanisms for such care (Directive 2011/24/EU 2011). Similarly, the Social Security Coordination Regulations 883/2004 facilitate cross-border labor mobility (Regulation 883/2004 n.d.).

A distinctive aspect of European CBC is the active participation of both governmental authorities at all levels and informal actors. Each of these groups occupies its own niche within the framework of cooperation. As previously discussed, the highest EU bodies play a key role in developing CBC mechanisms. National governments, regional and local authorities, and non-governmental actors each contribute to this multifaceted process, occupying distinct roles within it.

Despite the EU's political support for regionalism and multilevel governance, the central governments of member states continue to hold the most significant powers in regulating CBC. They oversee border regimes with regard to national security and economic policy, shape migration, customs, and taxation policies, establish the legal framework for cooperation, create intergovernmental commissions, play a key role in funding CBC programs, engage in strategic regional development planning, and exercise particularly strong authority over CBC in areas such as long-haul transport, healthcare, education, and crime prevention (Gomez Prieto 2016; Scott 2000). In many cases, regional authorities must coordinate their efforts in advancing CBC with central governments.

Defining the foundational frameworks of the European CBC still largely depends on bilateral or multilateral interstate arrangements, such as bilateral treaties on friendship and cooperation. Additionally, some bilateral or multilateral agreements (e.g., between Spain and Portugal, or Germany, France, Belgium, and Luxembourg) are specifically dedicated to CBC (Durand 2014).

Regional authorities often have a deeper understanding of local conditions than central governments, making them indispensable participants in CBC projects across various sectors and key contributors to their successful implementation (Eskelinen and Jukarainen 2000). In cases where CBC is coordinated by central governments, regional representatives actively participate in the work of intergovernmental commissions (Scott 2000). In the EU, regional authorities are central to the establishment of Euroregions as well as various cross-border interregional committees and the attraction of funding for Interreg projects (Sohn 2023). Since regions in different EU countries have varying powers depending on the degree of political centralization, asymmetries can arise in CBC. Regions in countries with more decentralized systems gain certain advantages and greater flexibility in their actions (Lange 2018).

Subregional authorities can play a pivotal role in implementing small-scale projects such as school partnerships, the establishment of museums, the preparation of informational materials, the organization of cultural and sports events, tourism initiatives, and more (Van Winsen 2009; Medeiros 2013). In some cases, these authorities utilize private-law contracts to bypass the need for higher-level government approval for engaging in international activities (Gabbe 2015). Subregional authorities play a vital role in representing the distinct needs and priorities of specific border communities, ensuring that CBC initiatives address the unique problems of these areas. Notably, the dominance of regional authorities can shift the focus of cooperation away from the immediate border zone to the broader region or to areas with greater economic or infrastructural potential (Terlouw 2012).

While official organizations establish formal institutional frameworks for cooperation, private actors—such as businesses, NGOs, and universities—often play a pivotal role in initiating and sustaining cross-border interactions (Calzada 2015). The activity, capacity, and willingness of private actors to cooperate, as well as the level of trust among them, are frequently decisive factors in mobilizing the potential of CBC and ultimately determining its effectiveness (Noferini et al. 2020).

The EU's cross-border cooperation CBC is far from perfect and is not immune to numerous problems and setbacks. One study, for instance, identified 239 obstacles to the European CBC (Rosanò 2021). According to research conducted by the Politecnico di Milano and cited during a public address by Ricardo Ferreira of the European Commission's Directorate-General for Regional and Urban Policy, removing 20% of the current legal and administrative barriers could lead to a 2% increase in GDP for EU cross-border regions and the creation of over 1 million jobs (European Commission 2024). Not all cross-border regions have achieved success though; some have shown only slow progress or stagnation (Kramsch 2003).

While internal borders between EU member states have largely ceased to serve as significant physical barriers to crossing, external EU borders remain a serious obstacle due to strict border controls. At the same time, internal borders still continue to pose substantial intangible barriers due to economic, legal, cultural, and other differences between neighboring countries. Such issues, even in the context of open borders, often result in more intensive network ties and cooperation among actors on the same side of the border compared to those across it. Paradoxically, in some cases, the intensity of cooperation decreases as border barriers are reduced. This can occur, for instance, when economic potentials between regions become more equal or when mutual familiarity between populations on either side of the border diminishes their interest in each other as partners (Spierings and Van Der Velde 2013).

It is unsurprising that European CBC faces numerous challenges, many of which are tied to intangible borders. These include linguistic and cultural differences (Yakhlef et al. 2017), poor accessibility of border regions due to geographical features or underdeveloped transportation networks, institutional and legal disparities (Engl and Evrard 2020), differences in the authority of regional governments (with some countries being more centralized than others), variations in taxation systems (Durand 2014), limited awareness of cross-border collaboration opportunities (Van Den Broek et al. 2020), depopulation of border areas (Balogh and Pete 2018), and restricted transport connectivity, among others. Additionally, CBC often encounters asymmetries, where one side possesses greater potential than the other. These imbalances can stem from disparities in funding, expertise, and experience, as well as from advantages in legal, administrative, fiscal, social, or other systems on one side of the border (Jauhiainen 2002).

The typical structural challenges of European CBC are further compounded by organizational issues. These include, for instance, insufficient organizational and legal frameworks for cooperation, which often render it legally non-binding (Decoville and Durand 2016); inadequate funding for initiatives and projects (Dimitrov et al. 2003); divergent goals and priorities among participants (Prokkola and Lois 2016); a lack of political will and interest in cooperation (Van Den Broek et al. 2020); insufficient mutual trust (O'Neill 2015); weak joint strategic vision and limited financial and other resources (Więckowski 2023); weak institutionalization (Knippschild and Wiechmann 2012); imbalances in resources, expertise, and authority between partners, leading to dominance by some over others (Koch 2015); uneven distribution of project funding (Perkmann 2007a); and a shift in cooperation priorities from border areas to regional administrative centers under the influence of central governments and economic lobbyists (Terlouw 2012). Other issues include the dominance of unaccountable bureaucrats and elites in cooperation processes, with limited involvement of non-governmental organizations and the general public (De Fátima Amante 2010); an overreliance on grants; corruption concerns (Rumelili 2005); and more. A frequently discussed problem is the insufficient engagement of non-governmental actors and the dominance of government actors, which often reduces cooperation to a formalized bureaucratic process or official paradiplomacy (Cressati et al. 2010; Noferini et al. 2020).

In some cases, the stability of CBC is threatened by crises in regional governments, which can lead to shifts in political priorities, budget cuts, and downsizing of departments responsible for CBC activities.

Intangible boundaries can also manifest as varying degrees of cautious perceptions toward the interests and values of the neighboring Other. Intensification of CBC, for instance, may raise concerns within official circles or among segments of the public. Cross-border cooperation based on economic disparities is not always viewed as economically beneficial or aligned with the interests of one side (Hansen 2000). In some cases, fears of fostering separatist tendencies may arise (Dodder and Faltan 1998).

While support for integration and a "Europe without borders" is generally high, CBC efforts occasionally encounter resistance from Euroskeptics and nationalist forces, who perceive such cooperation as a threat to national interests or identity (Yndigegn 2013). For example, German–Polish CBC has faced challenges stemming from negative historical memory and opposition from right-wing nationalist movements (Mirwaldt 2012). Historical grievances and nationalism also hinder CBC in other regions, such as the German–Danish borderlands (Hansen 2000).

Weakened border barriers and intensified cross-border flows with non-EU countries are sometimes perceived as threats to national security due to concerns over uncontrolled migration, smuggling, and related issues (Sallai and Jónás 2004). Moreover, cooperation with non-EU states is more vulnerable to disruption caused by diplomatic disagreements between central governments (Gkintidis 2013), particularly in the absence of an overarching authority like the EU to mediate on both sides of the border. The effectiveness of CBC along the EU's external borders can also be undermined by partners' perceptions of EU attempts to impose its conditions for cooperation, including the promotion of its values and border security frameworks, as a form of imperial policy (Dimitrovova 2012).

A distinctive type of EU CBC involves managing cooperation between communities in conflict. A key distinction is that CBC in conflict-affected areas demonstrates heightened sensitivity to potential conflicts arising from interactions between the parties, unlike typical cross-border cooperation. Given this sensitivity, some researchers argue that a consociational model is most appropriate for managing such cooperation. This approach advocates starting with carefully calibrated interactions in the least contentious areas, gradually increasing the intensity of cooperation over time (Anderson 2008).

The most prominent example of this sort of European CBC is the collaboration in the Northern Irish borderlands between Catholic and Protestant communities. Cross-border cooperation between the North and South of the island of Ireland intensified during the 1990s, driven by the establishment of the European Single Market and the introduction of funding programs for regional and cross-border cooperation. In 1993, the gradual removal of border checks along the Irish–British border began, concluding in 2005. That same year, the Joint Business Council was established, marking a pivotal step in advancing CBC on the island. The Council emerged as a joint initiative of the Irish Business and Employers Confederation and the Confederation of British Industry, the most influential British business organization. The aim of the Joint Business Council was to promote shared prosperity and employment growth by facilitating the movement of people, goods, services, energy, and investments across the island (Laffan and Payne 2003).

With financial support from the EU and later from the governments of both countries, the activities of subregional associations intensified during the 1990s and 2000s. These associations included the East Border Region (established in 1976), the Irish Central Border Areas Network (ICBAN, established in 1995), and the

2.2 European Union

North-West Region Cross Border Group. Comprising representatives of local authorities, these groups focused on fostering cross-border network connections among the governments of their respective local areas (Laffan and Payne 2003; Tannam 2006).

The Good Friday Agreement (GFA) or Belfast Agreement, signed in April 1998, established the legal framework for large-scale CBC supported by substantial financial backing from the EU, as well as the governments of the United Kingdom and Ireland. The agreement laid out principles and mechanisms for ending violence, enabling peaceful transformation, and governing Northern Ireland through consensus among key political forces within institutions such as the Northern Ireland Assembly and the Northern Ireland Executive. The GFA also created a range of institutions to facilitate cooperation both between Northern Ireland and Ireland ("North–South") and between Ireland and the United Kingdom ("East–West"). Key areas of cooperation under the North–South framework included veterinary and phytosanitary standards, teacher training and exchanges, transport planning, environmental protection, inland waterways, social security for cross-border workers, tourism, relevant EU programs, inland fisheries, aquaculture, emergency medical services, and urban and rural development (The Belfast Agreement 1998).

In 1999, within the North–South framework, InterTradeIreland was established with the aim of overcoming market segmentation on the island, fostering strategic alliances between Northern Irish and Irish firms, and jointly promoting Irish products abroad. The following year, in 2000, Tourism Ireland was created, with its primary objective being the joint marketing of the island as a unified tourist destination (Tannam 2006). By the 2010s, the two sides advanced to collaborative territorial planning in areas such as construction, transportation, infrastructure, and energy. A key milestone in this development was the 2013 Framework for Cooperation between the Republic of Ireland and Northern Ireland (Peel and Lloyd 2015; Framework for Co-Operation 2010).

Despite the strict control exerted by central governments over key directions of CBC, regional authorities still play a pivotal role. They bear the primary responsibility for implementing projects, with partnerships between local councils on either side of the border often serving as a prerequisite for receiving EU funding (Tannam 2007). In the 1990s, Northern Ireland saw the emergence of District Partnerships, composed of representatives from local authorities, community organizations, businesses, and educational institutions. These partnerships aimed to address the localized economic and social consequences of conflict and foster reconciliation between communities. In the 2000s, County Council-Led Task Forces (CCLTFs) began to emerge within broader cross-border associations of border counties in Ireland and Northern Ireland. These task forces placed a stronger emphasis on economic development (Buchanan 2008).

The Northern Irish experience of CBC in the context of conflict resolution stands out due to the remarkable levels of support for such projects from key stakeholders, including the governments of the United Kingdom and Ireland, as well as the European Union. The EU has been the largest donor, providing €1.6 billion to fund approximately 22,500 projects since 1995 under the PEACE programs (PEACE I,

PEACE II, PEACE III, and PEACE IV/Plus), with an additional €0.7 billion in co-financing from the Irish and Northern Irish governments (SEUPB n.d.).

Initially, these projects focused on supporting local initiatives and rebuilding community ties. Over time, however, the emphasis shifted toward addressing issues of economic development (Buchanan 2008). Since 1999, the program has been managed by the Special EU Programmes Body (SEUPB), an institution accountable to the European Commission and the governments of Ireland and Northern Ireland, with its status formalized under the 1998 Belfast Agreement. In addition to overseeing funding under the PEACE programs, the SEUPB also administers EU funds allocated to Northern Irish projects under the Interreg program, in which regional actors are eligible to participate. As part of EU-funded projects, recipients were required to provide co-financing amounting to at least 25% of the total project cost (Wilson 2000).

Brexit posed a serious challenge to both the peace process and CBC in Northern Ireland. Following complex negotiations, the UK and the EU agreed to maintain the framework for CBC, including funding through the Special EU Programmes Body. The preservation of key elements of cooperation—such as an open border and unhindered interaction between Northern Ireland and the EU's single market was enshrined in the Protocol on Ireland/Northern Ireland (Revised Protocol 2019). This protocol represented a major political concession by the UK, which accepted customs checks on goods moving from Great Britain to Northern Ireland to avoid jeopardizing the peace process. To implement the protocol, a pivotal role in Northern Irish CBC has been assumed by the Joint Committee on the Implementation of the Withdrawal Agreement, comprised of representatives from the UK and the EU and tasked with ensuring compliance with the agreements between the two parties.

Overall, cross-border cooperation between Northern Ireland and Ireland has yielded notable results, as acknowledged by respondents in several surveys. Interestingly, respondents from the Catholic community expressed significantly greater optimism about these outcomes than those from the Protestant community (Byrne et al. 2009).

Significant progress has been made in areas such as promoting trade, enhancing transport and communication links, developing electrical grids, advancing joint tourism initiatives across the island (McCall 2011), combating crime (Davies 2021), managing emergencies, improving healthcare and education (Hayward 2021), and organizing cultural and sports events (Lynch 2005). Already in the early years of CBC programs, tens of thousands of participants from the conflicting communities engaged in various initiatives. Particular emphasis was placed on supporting small-scale local projects that involved members of both communities (Buchanan 2008).

However, cross-border cooperation in Northern Ireland faces several significant challenges, many of which are directly or indirectly tied to the legacy of the conflict.

Firstly, certain political forces, particularly unionist groups, view cooperation with their traditional opponents with alarm, fearing that such collaboration might provide their opponents with economic or political advantages (Tannam 2006), potentially even leading to the absorption of Northern Ireland into Ireland (McCall and Itçaina 2017).

Secondly, organizers of CBC occasionally express concerns that intensified cooperation might, in some cases, provoke new intercommunity conflicts (Lynch 2005; Deiana et al. 2019).

Thirdly, Northern Irish CBC was established as a top-down initiative by central governments, which continue to play a dominant role as gatekeepers of the Belfast Agreements. This centralization often results in excessive bureaucratization and relegates local initiatives to a subordinate role (Tannam 2007; Laffan and Payne 2003), leaving local governments with only limited authority to establish cross-border connections.

Fourthly, the success of CBC has been limited, as cross-border trade between the two territories has not seen significant growth and continues to play a modest economic role, accounting for only about 5% of the trade of both Northern Ireland and Ireland (Bradley 2018). Moreover, Ireland's more dynamic economic growth compared to Northern Ireland creates an economic imbalance, reducing incentives for Irish entrepreneurs to engage in cross-border cooperation (Brooks et al. 2020).

Fifthly, some researchers criticize the focus of support on economic projects rather than reconciliation efforts, arguing that this approach merely reinforces existing ethnic divisions (Deiana et al. 2019). Additionally, EU-funded programs have been criticized for shifting their emphasis from the original goal of rebuilding social ties at the local community level to supporting economic development projects managed through more centralized mechanisms (Buchanan 2008).

It is important to note that the numerous challenges faced by CBC in the EU come to light not only because of their significance and urgency but also due to the extensive research devoted to them and the willingness of policymakers and experts to thoroughly identify and address them. The thorough exploration of shortcomings and barriers of CBC is a distinctive feature of the European experience, setting it apart from that of other countries and regions worldwide.

2.3 North America

The framework of cross-border cooperation (CBC) in North America, between the United States and its neighbors Canada and Mexico, differs fundamentally from that in the EU. In North America, CBC is not underpinned by a comprehensive integration project aimed at minimizing physical and virtual border barriers or fostering cross-border identities (Säre 2020). Full-fledged cross-border regionalism of the European model is not encouraged (as regions have very limited authority to enter into international agreements), nor is there generous support for CBC projects through multibillion-dollar joint grant programs. In the case of U.S.–Canada cooperation, shared language (though not shared identity) significantly facilitates CBC, while in the U.S.–Mexico border region, both English and Spanish are widely used across borders. Another key aspect of North American CBC is the dominance of the United

States, which wields vastly superior economic and political power compared to its neighbors and effectively advances its security and commercial interests.

The measures implemented by the United States to strengthen border security following the September 11, 2001, terrorist attacks significantly impacted the character of CBC in the region. In their 2000 study, Blatter and Clement highlighted the dominance of initiatives led by non-state actors, some of which wield strong lobbying power (Blatter and Clement 2000), while Scott emphasized the entrepreneurial focus of North American CBC (Scott 1999). The post-9/11 tightening of border security has substantially increased the role of central governments in CBC, although the initiatives of non-state actors remain significant—arguably even more so than in the EU, according to some researchers (Cappellano and Makkonen 2020).

The current agenda of North American CBC appears significantly narrower compared to its European counterpart, focusing primarily on mitigating the impacts of heightened border controls on cross-border traffic (especially trade) and supporting environmental projects. Both trade and environmental initiatives have received priority attention under the North American Free Trade Agreement (NAFTA) (Pipkin 2018a), signed in the 1990s and replaced by the United States–Mexico–Canada Agreement (USMCA) in 2020. It is important to note that the U.S. borders with Canada and Mexico are among the most frequently crossed heavily guarded borders in the world: approximately 100 million crossings are recorded annually on the U.S.–Canada border, and around 300–400 million on the U.S.–Mexico border (Bureau of Transportation Statistics, n.d.). The markedly higher mobility across the U.S.–Mexico border is attributed not only to Mexico's larger population but also to differences in wages and prices, which make the neighboring markets more attractive to one another (Cappellano and Rizzo 2019).

While U.S.–Canada security relations are characterized by a high level of trust, enabling the development of a shared security system with complementary components, the same cannot be said for U.S.–Mexico relations, where such trust is lacking, prompting the United States to rely on unilateral measures. Contributing to this disparity are the significant economic advantages of the United States and Canada over Mexico, as well as Mexico's much more centralized system of governance compared to its northern neighbors. The United States and Canada have substantially greater resources than Mexico to fund border infrastructure modernization projects. However, such funding, despite its considerable scale, is typically carried out in parallel (with each country addressing its own side of the border) rather than jointly.

Even before September 11, U.S.–Canada cooperation in border security, despite some differences, was grounded in a high level of mutual trust in the quality of each other's operations. This trust formed the foundation of the Smart Border Declaration, signed shortly after 9/11, which outlined the creation of a "smart border" that addressed both security needs and the necessity of maintaining robust economic ties between the two countries. The declaration identified key areas for bilateral security cooperation, with a commitment to decisive action to achieve these objectives (The White House 2002).

2.3 North America

In 2011, the leaders of Canada and the United States signed the Declaration on a Shared Vision for Perimeter Security and Economic Competitiveness, leading to the implementation of the Beyond the Border: A Shared Vision for Perimeter Security and Economic Competitiveness action plan. This plan prioritized joint efforts in areas such as early threat detection, cross-border law enforcement cooperation, facilitation of trade, promotion of economic growth and job creation, pre-inspection and pre-clearance initiatives, regulation of border fees, enhancement of cybersecurity, and more. Annual progress reports were mandated to assess the plan's outcomes (Public Safety Canada 2018).

These initiatives resulted in the establishment of a partially integrated U.S.–Canada system for immigration, customs control, and law enforcement.

Historically, the United States, Canada, and Mexico—particularly from the mid-twentieth century onward—normally have not implemented formal exit immigration and customs controls, viewing such measures as an unnecessary use of resources. Instead, information about departing travelers is typically collected through alternative means, such as airline records. However, as part of the Beyond the Border action plan, the United States and Canada launched the Entry/Exit Initiative, enabling the exchange of traveler information for those crossing the U.S.–Canada border (Government of Canada 2019). In 2015, the two countries signed the Preclearance Agreement, which allows both sides to conduct pre-clearance controls on each other's territory for passengers traveling via various modes of transport (Government of Canada n.d.). Under this arrangement, passengers who undergo pre-clearance at designated airports are exempt from immigration and customs checks upon arrival in the destination country.

Key mechanisms of the jointly developed system for managing cross-border flows of travelers and goods include programs tailored to frequent border crossers, whether carriers or individuals. In 2002, the Canada Border Services Agency and the U.S. Customs and Border Protection launched the Free and Secure Trade (FAST) program (U.S. Customs and Border Protection n.d.) and the NEXUS program (U.S. Customs and Border Protection n.d.).

FAST provides significant benefits to certified importers from Canada, the United States, and Mexico, such as exemption from routine inspections, access to dedicated border lanes, and relocation of certain control procedures outside border zones. Unlike their Canadian counterparts, Mexican importers can apply for FAST certification only through U.S. Customs and Border Protection, underscoring the asymmetry in U.S.–Mexico cross-border relations and a lack of mutual trust.

In a similar vein, NEXUS offers comparable benefits—dedicated lanes and expedited border clearance—to pre-approved individual travelers. For the U.S.–Mexico border, a partial equivalent to NEXUS is the SENTRI program, launched in 1995 at the San Diego border crossing and later expanded to other locations. Unlike NEXUS, SENTRI is administered exclusively by U.S. authorities.

To alleviate the impact of heightened security measures on cross-border flows, dialogue with businesses and the public on border management issues was established. As part of this effort, the United States and Canada launched the Transportation Border Working Group (TBWG) in 2002 to address challenges such as border congestion, cross-border transportation infrastructure development, and informing businesses about border crossing regulations. Meeting twice a year, the TBWG includes representatives from government agencies, regional and municipal authorities, chambers of commerce, businesses, and other stakeholders, as well as transportation experts. Additionally, the group operates subcommittees that meet more frequently to focus on specific areas such as data, technology, and communication (Conroy 2011).

To address border congestion, both countries place significant emphasis on developing cross-border transportation infrastructure. These efforts are carried out in parallel but in coordination, supported by national infrastructure funding programs with multibillion-dollar budgets (Border Policy Research Institute 2014a). To identify the causes of border delays, cross-border traffic is periodically monitored in collaboration with research institutions such as the Border Policy Research Institute at Western Washington University (Border Policy Research Institute 2011).

One of the key areas of cooperation on border security has been the establishment of close collaboration between U.S. and Canadian law enforcement agencies to combat illegal cross-border activities. As early as 1996, the creation of multipurpose Border Enforcement Teams was initiated for this purpose, later expanding significantly after September 11. A unique mechanism was introduced with the signing of the 2009 Integrated Cross-Border Maritime Law Enforcement Operations Initiative (commonly known as the Shiprider Agreement). This agreement authorized joint teams to conduct operations across the border without undergoing standard border control procedures and granted officers from both countries the authority to enforce their national laws on the other country's territory (Framework Agreement 2009).

The comprehensive efforts by North American governments to enhance border security alongside optimizing the management of cross-border traffic have not fully mitigated the effects of heightened border controls implemented after September 11. By the late 2010s, traffic across the U.S.–Canada border had decreased by approximately one-third compared to the 1990s, and by around 30% across the U.S.–Mexico border (Bureau of Transportation Statistics n.d.).

North American cross-border traffic management projects continue to face several significant challenges, including divergent priorities between the United States and its neighbors (the United States prioritizes security, while its partners emphasize trade) (Leuprecht et al. 2021); insufficient trust between the parties, particularly at the U.S.–Mexico border, where U.S. policies often take a unilateral approach (Border Policy Research Institute 2014b); the vulnerability of cooperation to political shifts (Hale 2011; Dupeyron 2017), exemplified by the Trump administration's stricter policies on migration and protectionism toward neighboring countries (Trautman et al. 2019); generally stringent U.S. immigration policies toward nationals of neighboring countries (Cappellano et al. 2021); differing national regulatory regimes for cross-border traffic control (Globerman and Storer 2014; Broadhurst and Trautman 2023), which often leave U.S. neighbors acting as policy-takers in response to American regulations (Hale 2019); asynchronous government funding cycles for border management and insufficient consideration of local conditions at specific regions and border crossings (Border Policy Research Institute 2008; Broadhurst and Trautman

2023); issues related to uneven distribution of cross-border traffic across entry points, seasonal fluctuations, and disparities in the modernization of border infrastructure (Border Policy Research Institute 2013, 2016); and inequities in funding opportunities among border crossings within the same country or between neighboring nations (e.g., U.S. crossings, unlike their Canadian counterparts, are permitted to collect fees and receive funding from regional authorities) (Melious 2006).

Facilitating cross-border traffic, along with fostering trade, employment, mobility, innovation, and tackling shared environmental challenges, is equally a key priority for regional cross-border cooperation.

The regions of Canada, Mexico, and the United States lack broad authority to engage in foreign policy, and any legally binding agreements they enter into with international partners—such as the 1992 Environmental Cooperation Agreement between Washington State and British Columbia (Environmental Cooperation Agreement 1992)—must be approved by the central government. Section 10 of Article 1 of the U.S. Constitution explicitly prohibits states from entering into agreements with foreign entities without Congressional consent. To circumvent these limitations, regions or cities often opt to sign non-legally binding memorandums of understanding with foreign partners, which, in practice, are frequently concluded following consultations with central authorities. Examples of such agreements include those between San Diego and Tijuana or Washington State and British Columbia. Additionally, cooperation is often carried out through formats like binational economic forums and coalitions (Border Policy Research Institute 2019) (Fig. 2.2).

It is worth noting that while U.S. and Canadian regions lack extensive authority for international engagement, they enjoy significant autonomy in domestic affairs and substantial financial independence. This enables them to coordinate synchronously with neighboring regions across the border in implementing projects, such as infrastructure initiatives, within their respective territories.

Regional cross-border cooperation initiatives face several additional challenges, including reliance on funding from central governments (which is often unstable), weak horizontal linkages between cities, and a lack of coordinated efforts in cross-border planning (Cappellano et al. 2021). Despite these challenges, regional and local authorities play a crucial role as coordinators and facilitators of communication and collaboration among various stakeholders, including private and non-governmental organizations (Leuprecht et al. 2021; Clauson and Trautman 2016).

Cross-border cooperation has been particularly active in the northwestern part of the U.S.–Canada border since the 1990s, especially between the U.S. state of Washington and the Canadian province of British Columbia. This collaboration is bolstered by a relatively strong shared identity within the "Cascadia region," to the extent that even separatist movements have emerged advocating for the region's independence as a sovereign state outside the United States and Canada. While cross-border initiatives also exist in the central and eastern parts of the U.S.–Canada border (such as in the Detroit-Windsor and Buffalo-Niagara Falls areas), they tend to be less extensive, integrated, and stable (Border Policy Research Institute and University of Buffalo Regional Institute 2009).

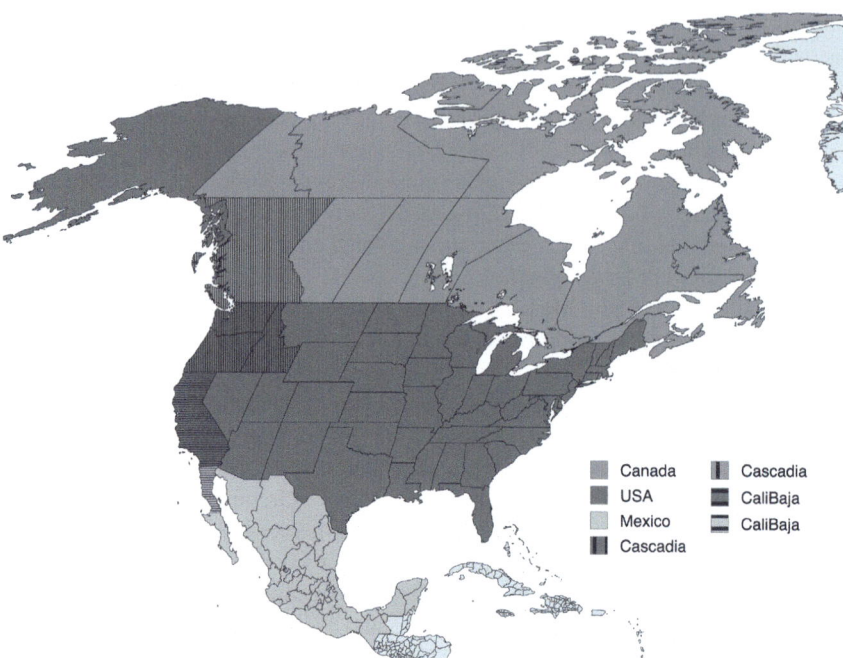

Fig. 2.2 North American states, their administrative regions, and cross-border regionalism

The most extensive North American regional cross-border organization along the U.S.–Canada border is the Future Borders Coalition, which comprises dozens of private organizations (primarily in transportation, cargo and logistics, and tourism sectors) as well as the government of Quebec. The coalition aims to advocate for optimal border policies, with its activities largely focused on developing recommendations for government agencies (Future Borders Coalition n.d.).

The cross-border cooperation carried out under the framework of the Pacific NorthWest Economic Region (PNWER), established in 1991 and headquartered in Seattle, takes on a more diverse and project-oriented nature. PNWER addresses economic, social, and environmental issues such as transportation, agriculture, innovation, labor markets, water resources, and emergency management, as well as lobbying shared interests in the capitals of both countries. Canadian participation includes the provinces and territories of British Columbia, Alberta, Saskatchewan, Yukon, and Northwest Territories, while U.S. participants include the states of Washington, Idaho, Montana, and Oregon. Functioning as a cross-border forum for both public authorities and the private sector, PNWER operates through 20 working groups, where private-sector representatives play a significant role. The organization is managed by compact governing bodies—the Executive Committee, Delegate Council, and Private Sector Council (Pacific NorthWest Economic Region n.d.)—and operates on a modest budget of less than $2 million.

2.3 North America

The International Mobility and Trade Corridor Program (IMTC) focuses primarily on issues related to the management of cross-border transportation infrastructure and traffic flows. Established in 1997 in the region between Washington State and the Canadian province of British Columbia, the program is a binational initiative involving federal, regional, and local government agencies from both the United States and Canada, as well as businesses, universities, and non-governmental organizations. Notably, the program is managed by one side—the Whatcom Council of Governments—a forum originally created to coordinate joint activities among local governments in Washington State, which later expanded its role to include transportation planning. This asymmetry in leadership could be attributed to the Council's demonstrated effectiveness and its greater administrative capacity compared to its Canadian counterparts.

Led by a Steering Committee that convenes monthly, the IMTC Program includes representatives from dozens of organizations, predominantly governments at various levels. Between 1997 and 2020, IMTC secured over $41 million in funding, primarily from the U.S. Federal Highway Administration for specific infrastructure projects, as well as from federal and municipal governments in both the United States and Canada. Among its donors is a private entity—the Bill & Melinda Gates Foundation (IMTC n.d.).

The Cascadia Innovation Corridor (CIC) initiative (Trautman et al. 2019) prioritizes pooling the innovative potential of neighboring regions to foster their collective development. Launched in 2016 by Microsoft, the initiative gained legitimacy through a memorandum of understanding between the governments of British Columbia and Washington State. CIC aims to promote economic growth and innovation while encouraging cross-border collaboration among regional governments, businesses, and universities. Key areas of focus include transportation, high-tech, clean energy, data analytics, and addressing climate change.

One of the first projects under CIC was the establishment of the Cascadia Urban Analytics Cooperative (CUAC) in 2017 by the University of British Columbia and the University of Washington. Supported by $1 million in funding from Microsoft, CUAC conducts research on urban development challenges, such as transportation, homelessness, and healthcare. In the same year, the governments of British Columbia, Washington State, and Oregon launched the Cascadia Venture Acceleration Network (CVAN), which involves 50 organizations, including universities, incubators, investors, and industry associations. CVAN's mission is to provide financial and informational support to cross-border startups in these priority areas (The University of British Columbia n.d.; Cappellano 2019).

Interregional cooperation along the U.S.–Mexico border faces significantly less favorable conditions compared to the U.S.–Canada border. Key obstacles include stricter border control and immigration policies, a lack of mutual trust between the parties, a more pronounced dominance of the United States in comparison to the relatively balanced dynamics of U.S.–Canada cooperation, weaker authority of Mexican regional governments compared to their American counterparts (Pipkin 2018b), and high crime rates on the Mexican side, among other challenges.

Despite these challenges, several interregional initiatives continue to develop. One notable example is the Cali Baja Initiative, launched in 2008 to promote economic partnerships between Southern California and the Mexican state of Baja California. The initiative focuses on industrial manufacturing, trade, biotechnology, clean energy, logistics, tourism, workforce development, and cultural exchange. Participants include local government agencies, businesses, universities, and research institutions. The initiative operates as a network without a centralized governing body, coordinating efforts primarily through joint projects (Tijuana EDC 2020). The management of the initiative exhibits an asymmetrical structure, with the U.S. side tending to dominate. A pivotal role is played by the San Diego Association of Governments (SANDAG), particularly through its Binational Borders Committee, where Mexican officials, such as representatives from the Consulate General of Mexico, participate as advisory members (San Diego Association of Governments, n.d.). Additionally, SANDAG contributes to cross-border planning in areas like transportation and environmental sustainability (Herzog and Sohn 2019).

The prominent role of environmental initiatives in North American cross-border cooperation can be attributed to several factors: long-standing traditions of environmental activism, a history of addressing transboundary river issues, and the emphasis placed on environmental concerns in the broader context of North American integration. Some researchers note a significant increase in the number of environmental NGOs in recent decades within the U.S.–Canada border region, as well as the intensification of cross-border collaborations among these organizations (Moscato 2023).

Environmental issues have played a significant role in shaping cross-border environmental initiatives, largely due to the prominence given to ecological concerns within the framework of NAFTA. Alongside NAFTA, Canada, Mexico, and the United States signed the North American Agreement on Environmental Cooperation (NAAEC), which came into effect in 1994. This agreement aimed to mitigate the environmental impacts of economic integration and led to the establishment of the Commission for Environmental Cooperation (CEC) to oversee its implementation. Additionally, the North American Development Bank (NADBANK) and the grant program North American Partnership for Environmental Community Action (NAPECA) have supported local community environmental efforts, with typical grants ranging from tens to hundreds of thousands of dollars. The NAAEC also empowered environmental organizations and individual activists in North America to file complaints against member states for failing to comply with its provisions.

However, critics point to the limited authority of the CEC (Mumme and Duncan 1996). Furthermore, the heightened border security measures introduced after September 11, 2001, have posed challenges for cross-border environmental activism (Stefanick 2009), while shifting political priorities have resulted in reduced U.S. funding for environmental initiatives. On the Mexican side of the U.S.–Mexico border, environmental activists face particularly severe challenges, including inadequate funding and governance, compounded by security threats posed by drug cartels in some cases (Herzog and Sohn 2019).

2.3 North America

North American cooperation in addressing the challenges of transboundary rivers has particularly deep roots, initially emerging as a mechanism for resolving border-related disputes and gradually evolving to incorporate a strong environmental protection dimension.

As early as 1889, the United States and Mexico established the International Boundary and Water Commission (IBWC) to address issues related to transboundary water bodies. Initially tasked with ensuring the accuracy of border demarcations along shared rivers, its mandate expanded in 1944 to include addressing environmental challenges such as water quality, biodiversity, and river infrastructure management between the two countries. The commission operates through closely coordinated efforts, with representatives from both nations meeting at least once a week.

A broader range of environmental issues in the U.S.–Mexico border region is managed by the Border Environment Cooperation Commission (BECC), headquartered in Ciudad Juárez, Mexico. Established in 1994 by the governments of the two countries, BECC focuses on a variety of cross-border environmental concerns.

In the U.S.–Canada border region, water management issues have been overseen since 1909 by the International Joint Commission (IJC), established under the intergovernmental Boundary Waters Treaty of the same year. Initially focused on resolving border disputes, the commission's responsibilities later expanded to include approving projects that alter water levels and addressing environmental challenges. The IJC is composed of six commissioners, three from each country, supported by subcommittees dedicated to specific sections of the border waters or particular issues, as well as technical staff. Additionally, the commission monitors air pollution in border regions (International Joint Commission 2018).

To jointly manage the biodiversity and water quality of the Great Lakes, prevent overfishing, and combat invasive species (notably, sea lampreys), the Great Lakes Fishery Commission was established in 1954 under the Convention on Great Lakes Fisheries (Great Lakes Fishery Commission n.d.). Furthermore, in 1961, the Columbia River Treaty was signed, facilitating the construction of three dams in British Columbia and one in Montana, as well as the management of energy generated by these dams (Treaty Relating to Cooperative Development 1961). Over time, greater emphasis has been placed on engaging civil society activists to oversee treaty compliance (Davidson 2014; Border Policy Research Institute 2017).

The activities of non-governmental environmental initiatives in the U.S.–Canada border region also have a long history. For instance, the establishment of international parks, such as the Waterton-Glacier International Peace Park and the Peace Arch Park, can be traced back to the efforts of environmental activists on both sides of the border during the nineteenth and early twentieth centuries. It is important to note that these and similar parks are not unified transboundary territories. Instead, they consist of adjacent national parks on either side of the border, working collaboratively to coordinate efforts for environmental conservation and biodiversity preservation (Timothy 1999).

One of the largest transboundary conservation initiatives in North America is the Yellowstone to Yukon Conservation Project (Y2Y). This project spans a corridor of over 3000 km across the U.S.–Canada border and is spearheaded by a broad coalition of environmental organizations operating on both sides of the border. The coalition has successfully advocated for the expansion of protected areas—between 1993 and 2018, the size of these areas increased by more than 80%. Additionally, the initiative focuses on ensuring wildlife connectivity through lands used for economic activities, promoting sustainable coexistence (Y2Y 2024; Stefanick 2009).

A notable example of an environmental initiative in the U.S.–Canada border region is the construction and conservation of the Salish Sea—a system of straits and channels located between the Canadian province of British Columbia and the U.S. state of Washington. The term "Salish Sea," later officially recognized in both countries, was first proposed in 1988 by Bert Webber, a professor at Western Washington University, to raise public awareness about the need for ecological protection in the area (Freelan n.d.). Since then, the Salish Sea has served as the geographical focus for various conservation projects (Säre 2020).

A distinctive focus of CBC involves protecting the interests of the indigenous First Nations population. Indigenous organizations are consistently invited to participate in cross-border initiatives to ensure their voices are heard. A pivotal role is played by the 1794 Jay Treaty, which grants indigenous peoples the right to move freely between neighboring countries while retaining their social rights. Although Canada does not fully recognize this treaty, some Canadian educational institutions waive tuition fees for First Nations representatives (Boos et al. 2014; O'Shea 2023).

2.4 China

With the longest land border in the world (over 22,000 km) and the largest number of neighboring states (14), alongside Russia, China stands as one of the most economically and politically powerful nations globally. Since the 1990s, external relations, particularly with neighboring countries, have played a pivotal role in China's economic policy. Initially, these efforts were driven by the Go Out Strategy, which aimed to promote the overseas activity of Chinese companies. Since the 2010s, they have been further advanced through the Belt and Road Initiative, focused on establishing transcontinental economic corridors. The Chinese model of cross-border cooperation, shaped under these conditions, reflects the country's growing economic power, its rigidly authoritarian political regime, and the central government's strategic use of its border potential, selectively granting substantial autonomy to local authorities for fostering cooperation (Fig. 2.3).

The first key component of China's model is the establishment of Cross-Border Economic Cooperation Zones (CBECZs). While the first special economic zones were created in China's coastal cities in the 1970s, their application to cross-border cooperation—particularly with Kazakhstan, Mongolia, Russia, and Vietnam—began in the 1990s. The Belt and Road Initiative in the 2010s provided further impetus for the development of additional CBECZs. A typical CBECZ structure involves adjacent territories on either side of the border, each under their respective national

2.4 China

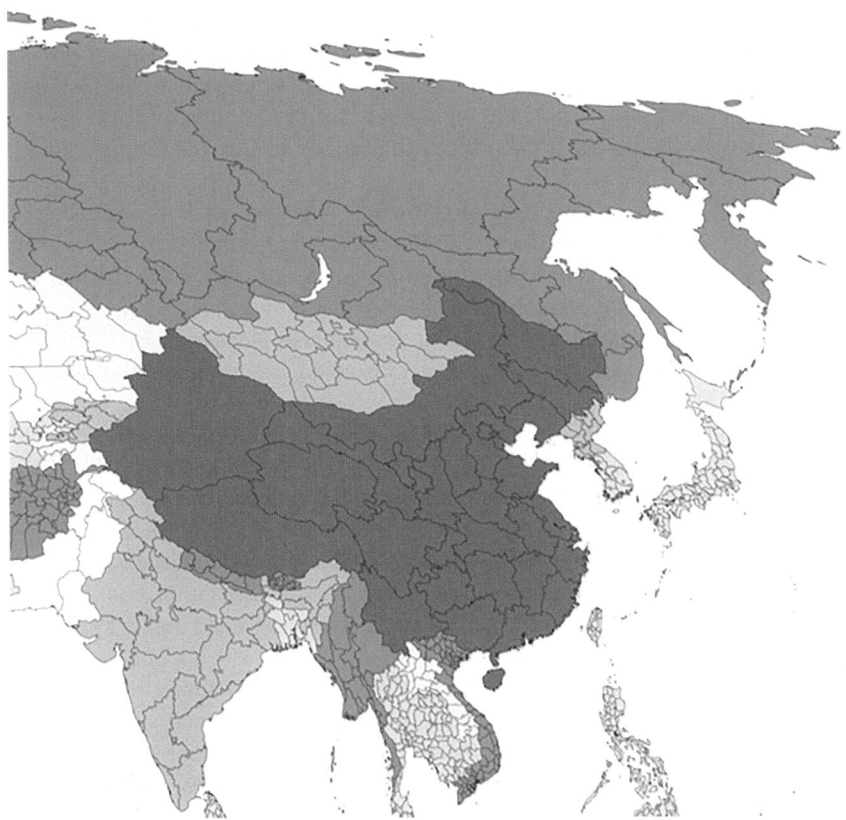

Fig. 2.3 China and its regions

jurisdictions. These zones are connected by robust infrastructure and operate under favorable migration and customs regimes, facilitating the movement of people and goods across the border (Pestsov and Volynchuk 2020).

China has been a global pioneer in the large-scale implementation of Cross-Border Economic Cooperation Zones (CBECZs). Its experience, albeit with varying degrees of success, has subsequently inspired similar initiatives in several other countries, including some ASEAN member states and Russia.

The second, even more ambitious component of China's cross-border cooperation model involves the empowerment of selected regions by the central government. These regions are granted additional powers and financial resources—particularly for implementing cross-border and transboundary projects—along with priority communication channels with the central authorities. At the same time, the central government maintains strict oversight of the regions' international activities, requiring approval for key initiatives in this domain (Su 2013).

The central authorities play a crucial role in establishing framework agreements for cooperation with neighboring countries, most of which also operate under authoritarian regimes. These agreements create a favorable environment for fostering cross-border cooperation, effectively giving it a green light. Moreover, the central government typically serves as the primary funding source for major infrastructure projects.

Since the 2010s, many Chinese regions have been under particular pressure to align their cross-border cooperation plans with the overarching Belt and Road Initiative (BRI) strategy. Such alignment often promises access to substantial funding for cross-border infrastructure development (Pestsov and Volynchuk 2020). However, this approach presents challenges: tailoring development plans to fit BRI priorities may lead to inefficiencies, mismanagement, or even misuse of funds (Peyrouse and Raballand 2015).

Building on this framework, regional authorities are further empowered to propose large-scale initiatives for developing cross-border cooperation, which require approval from the central government. These initiatives may include the establishment of cross-border economic zones, development of transboundary infrastructure, and the creation of joint governance institutions with adjacent territorial entities. Examples include the Guangdong-Hong Kong Cooperation Joint Conference, although the effectiveness of such bodies is not always rated highly by experts (Smart and Lin 2004). Regional authorities are also tasked with adopting programs for fostering cross-border cooperation, maintaining regular communication with their counterparts across the border, organizing business missions, and similar activities. To oversee cross-border collaboration in specific sectors, steering groups are often established within Chinese regions. These groups typically consist of officials specialized in the relevant fields from the respective departments of local administrations (Su 2013).

The empowering of those borderland provinces that could demonstrate the potential effectiveness of their plans to the central government became a significant component of China's regional policy. This policy aimed at revitalizing and stimulating the economic development of peripheral areas, which had been marginalized during the period of isolation (Pestsov and Volynchuk 2020).

In some cases, the strategy of granting regions special powers was employed to alleviate partners' concerns about China's potential dominance in cross-border cooperation. This approach was utilized in China's participation in the Greater Mekong Subregion initiative, established in 1992, which included Cambodia, Laos, Myanmar, Thailand, and Vietnam, along with China's Yunnan Province. In 2005, the initiative was expanded to include the Guangxi Zhuang Autonomous Region (Su 2013). A similar strategy was applied to facilitate the reintegration of Hong Kong, handed back to China by the United Kingdom in 1997 under the condition of maintaining broad economic and political autonomy until 2047. To address Hong Kong's concerns over the political implications and economic disparities of extensive economic cooperation with China, its primary economic partner became the neighboring Guangdong Province (Yang 2006).

The Chinese model of cross-border cooperation has delivered mixed results. On the one hand, China has become at least one of the priority partners for nearly all its neighboring states, with the exception of Bhutan, and its ties with these countries have become increasingly multifaceted and dynamic. The delegation of extensive powers to local authorities has fostered their initiative, which in some cases (such as Guangdong-Hong Kong cooperation) has led to innovative approaches in infrastructure development, technology, and environmental protection (Shen 2004).

This cooperation has, in certain instances, resulted in impressive projects, such as the Hong Kong-Zhuhai-Macao Bridge, the world's longest sea bridge at 55 km, inaugurated in 2018. Another notable example is the Hong Kong-Shenzhen Innovation and Technology Park, launched in 2017. This initiative has effectively merged the capacities of high-tech industries with R&D advancements through collaborations with local universities (Kang and Jiang 2020). In the northern border city of Heihe, the Cross-Border E-Commerce Park, operational since 2012, has become a pivotal logistics hub, attracting companies involved in online trade between Russia and China and significantly contributing to the city's economic growth (Mikhailova 2018).

Another interesting case is the Khorgos Special Economic Zone, notable for its preferential tax regime, which offers tax breaks, reduced tariffs, and streamlined customs procedures to attract investment and promote trade. Situated on the border with Kazakhstan in China's Xinjiang Uighur Autonomous Region, the zone features the Khorgos International Center for Boundary Cooperation (ICBC), including a joint free trade zone. This center held particular significance prior to the recent reciprocal implementation of visa-free travel between China and Kazakhstan, as it facilitated visa-free entry for traders and tourists. Of particular importance is the Khorgos Gateway Dry Port, a logistics hub on the Kazakhstan-China border, inaugurated in 2015. It spans 129.8 hectares and features advanced infrastructure, including logistics and industrial zones, the capacity to store up to 18,000 containers, and gantry cranes for seamless cargo transfers between China's standard rail gauge (1435 mm) and Kazakhstan's rail gauge (1520 mm). Its importance has grown with the increased significance of the Middle Corridor as an alternative to the Northern Corridor through Russia. The development of Khorgos began during Hu Jintao's tenure, though its strategic relevance was greatly elevated under the Belt and Road Initiative (BRI). As Xinjiang was designated a "core region" (*hexin qu*) within the Silk Road Economic Belt, the BRI's land-based component (Belt and Road Forum for International Cooperation 2017), this initiative emphasized domestic development to address economic disparities between the more developed eastern provinces and the less developed western regions, such as Xinjiang, maintaining a coherent focus on national growth.

On the other hand, China's model of cross-border cooperation often reflects its overwhelming economic power and unilateral efforts, which are insufficiently matched by equivalent commitments from its partners. These gaps include deficiencies in infrastructure development, legal frameworks, and the delegation of authority to regional governments for cross-border projects. Many of China's neighbors involved in cross-border cooperation face governance challenges, with their systems often more bureaucratic and corrupt than China's (Tochkov 2022). For instance, China's cooperation with Russia and Myanmar is hindered by centralized and rigid decision-making processes in these countries (Pestsov 2021; Kosonen et al. 2008). In Russia, slow implementation of infrastructure projects further complicates progress. Additionally, both China and many of its neighboring countries struggle with high levels of corruption. This poses risks to the successful execution of joint infrastructure and other projects, particularly given the lack of transparency in fund allocation mechanisms (Peyrouse and Raballand 2015).

Despite efforts to strike an optimal balance between a centralized political system and the encouragement of local initiative, the authoritarian nature of this system often negatively impacts the dynamics of cooperation. In particular, it can become overly bureaucratic, leaving insufficient room for the involvement of non-state actors, especially in areas beyond the economic sphere, such as environmental protection and education (Chu and Lee 2019).

China's attempts to alleviate partners' concerns about its dominance in cross-border cooperation have not always been sufficient. While support for such cooperation has grown significantly in neighboring regions, alarmist sentiments regarding China's expanding influence remain strong (Pestsov and Volynchuk 2020). Such concerns were a driving force behind the series of mass protests in Kazakhstan in 2016 against amendments to the Land Code, which allowed foreigners to lease land for extended periods (BBC News 2016). Similarly, Guangdong's cooperation with Hong Kong has faced resistance from some Hongkongers due to the intensified influx of migrants from Mainland China, which has sharply increased the strain on Hong Kong's social services and driven up housing prices (Yang and Li 2013).

The lack of a lingua franca for official and informal interactions between China and its neighboring partners also negatively impacts cross-border cooperation. Efforts by both sides to promote mutual language learning—such as express courses in Russian for Chinese officials and entrepreneurs in the China–Russia border region—often prove insufficient. This inadequacy affects not only the quality of communication during interactions but also the exchange of information about potential opportunities for cooperation (Kashin and Yankova 2021).

2.5 Southeast Asia

The Association of Southeast Asian Nations (ASEAN), established in 1967, is often regarded as one of the most successful regional integration frameworks. Despite significant economic, political, and cultural differences among its members, it has achieved notable milestones since the 1990s, including the establishment of a free trade area and the development of a distinctive consensus-based decision-making mechanism that accommodates the divergent interests of its diverse membership. ASEAN's accomplishments and legal frameworks, such as the free trade area, cooperation in border management (ASEAN 2021), and the creation of a virtual platform to facilitate cross-border connections among small and medium-sized enterprises

2.5 Southeast Asia

Fig. 2.4 Association of Southeast Asian Nations (ASEAN)

(ASEAN 2023), have, to some extent, fostered cross-border cooperation in certain areas (Fig. 2.4).

The diversity among ASEAN member states, coupled with the bloc's prioritization of consensus-building, nevertheless often significantly hampers the development of unified policies across various domains. This explains why cross-border cooperation occupies a relatively minor position in ASEAN's official discourse, even though related areas, such as the standardization of border management and the promotion of cross-border trade, have seen considerable progress.

The nature of cross-border cooperation largely depends on the specific characteristics and policies of the cooperating ASEAN member states. Importantly, ASEAN countries vary substantially in their economic capacities (with Singapore, Brunei, Malaysia, and Thailand significantly outpacing Indonesia, Vietnam, and the Philippines, and even more so Cambodia and Myanmar in GDP per capita), levels of democratic governance (Indonesia and the Philippines are more democratic, followed by Malaysia, Singapore, and Thailand, while the remaining ASEAN members are classified as authoritarian regimes), and degrees of political decentralization. Indonesia's regions enjoy the broadest powers, followed by Malaysia, particularly in Borneo, and the Philippines, which, while lacking land borders, has notable regional autonomy. In contrast, the other ASEAN countries maintain highly centralized governance systems.

It is unsurprising that, as characterized by Nadalutti and Rüland, ASEAN's cross-border cooperation is generally marked by a high degree of centralization and a predominantly top-down approach, functioning more as a tool for development than for fostering regional cohesion (Nadalutti and Rüland 2024). Within this framework, regions typically play a subordinate role, acting as implementers of centrally imposed decisions. Notable exceptions include Indonesia–Malaysia cross-border cooperation on the island of Borneo (Kalimantan), where regions in both countries enjoy considerable autonomy, at least in domestic policy matters, and Indonesia–Singapore cross-border cooperation, where, due to the small geographical size of Singapore, the distinction between national and regional authorities is virtually absent.

The diversity of governance systems among ASEAN member states complicates the standardization of cooperation practices and poses challenges to ensuring compliance with agreed-upon norms in areas such as border management (Plümmer 2022). Furthermore, challenges related to the absence of a common lingua franca frequently arise during project implementation. Efforts to promote English as a regional working language have not always been sufficient to overcome these issues (Bruthiaux 2008).

The most common tools of ASEAN cross-border cooperation are growth triangles or areas, as well as free trade zones modeled after China's cross-border cooperation practices. Additionally, one of the key cross-border cooperation initiatives involving ASEAN countries and several other stakeholders is the Greater Mekong Subregion (GMS).

The growth triangle model envisions the pooling of competitive advantages of adjacent territories (e.g., affordable labor, investments, and natural resources) from neighboring countries. Pioneers of the growth triangle format, typically encompassing border and nearby areas of neighboring nations, included Singapore, Malaysia, and Indonesia. The SIJORI Triangle, initiated in 1989 by Singapore, brought together Singapore, the Malaysian state of Johor, and the Indonesian Riau Islands, aiming to establish production chains and new jobs, encourage investments, and develop infrastructure and tourism (Karim et al. 2024). Similar goals, with some modifications, were pursued by the Indonesia–Malaysia–Thailand Growth Triangle established in 1993, the Brunei–Indonesia–Malaysia–Philippines East ASEAN Growth Area launched in 1994, and the Cambodia–Laos–Vietnam Development Triangle Area introduced in 1999 (Nadalutti and Rüland 2024).

While all these growth triangles or areas achieved some degree of success, the SIJORI Triangle stood out as the most successful, reflecting the relatively higher levels of economic development and governance democratization of its participating countries. In contrast, the other initiatives faced more significant challenges related to investments, infrastructure, and bureaucratic hurdles. Researchers also highlight common issues inherent to growth triangles: cooperation often focuses on bilateral rather than multilateral ties, while distrust and suspicions over the distribution of benefits have occasionally strained relations between partners within the triangles (Nadalutti and Rüland 2024).

Since the late 1990s, certain ASEAN member states, including Thailand, Vietnam, Myanmar, and Laos, began establishing cross-border trade or industrial zones. These zones featured simplified customs procedures and reduced tariffs aimed at stimulating the development of border regions where small-scale trade played a vital role in the livelihoods of local populations. The systematic creation of such zones gained particular importance in the 2000s as part of Thailand's policy to balance regional economic development. This strategy involved redistributing investments and trade flows to benefit peripheral areas while fostering cooperation with less affluent neighboring countries, including employing low-cost labor in border zones (Anuar and Harun 2018).

These priorities were reflected in Thailand's adoption of the Ayeyawady–Chao Phraya–Mekong Economic Cooperation Strategy (ACMECS) in 2003. The overarching goal of this initiative was to bridge the economic development gap between Thailand and its less developed neighbors—Cambodia, Laos, Myanmar, and Vietnam—through joint cross-border growth initiatives (Krainara and Routray 2015). Thailand's cross-border cooperation also extended to other areas, such as joint educational and exchange programs for schools in adjacent border regions, including English language instruction to establish it as a lingua franca for cross-border interactions (Kaewkumkong and Sen 2019).

The Greater Mekong Subregion (GMS) initiative, launched by the Asian Development Bank in 1992, geographically encompasses territories within the Mekong River Basin, including five ASEAN member states—Cambodia, Laos, Thailand, Myanmar, and Vietnam—as well as two Chinese territories: Yunnan Province and, since 2002, the Guangxi Zhuang Autonomous Region. Its priorities include fostering economic development, strengthening infrastructure connectivity (notably through transport corridors), environmental protection, water management, agriculture, tourism, education, and healthcare (Fig. 2.5).

This program, which also involves regions, intergovernmental and non-governmental organizations, businesses, and international donors, lacks formal membership, official status, or a clear governance structure. Strategic and major project-related decisions are made at the GMS Ministerial Conference and the GMS Leaders' Summit, while implementation and ongoing oversight in specific sectors—such as environmental protection, transportation, tourism, energy, and healthcare—are handled by working groups and sectoral committees. Secretariat functions are carried out by the Asian Development Bank, which initiated the project.

The GMS initiative has achieved several tangible outcomes, particularly in strengthening regional connectivity, developing transportation infrastructure, and promoting economic corridors (North–South, East–West, and South)—zones situated along key transportation routes (Tangseefa 2018; Anuar and Harun 2018). Over the course of its implementation, the initiative has facilitated investments exceeding $20 billion (Greater Mekong Subregion n.d.). One of its most significant agreements is the 1999 Cross-Border Transport Facilitation Agreement, aimed at harmonizing laws, procedures, and requirements for the movement of goods, vehicles, and people across regional borders (Krainara and Routray 2015). However, the initiative has faced substantial criticism for its inability to prevent environmental degradation, prioritizing economic growth at the expense of sustainability, and lacking clear governance mechanisms and stable funding (Bruthiaux 2008).

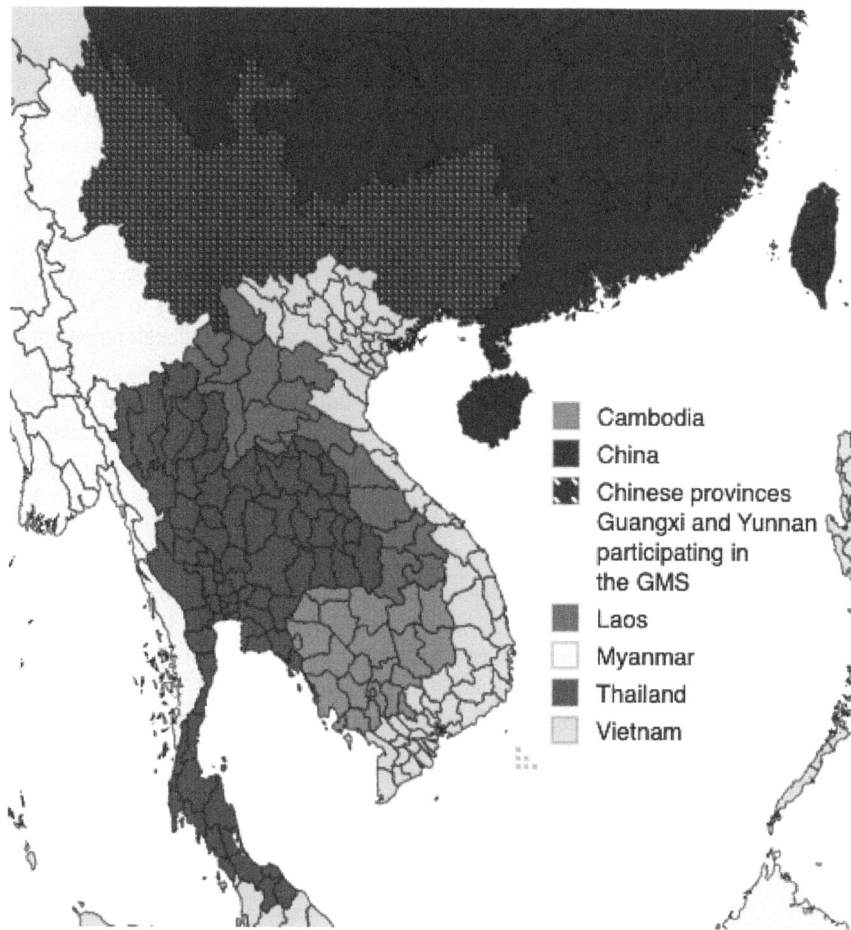

Fig. 2.5 States and regions participating in the Greater Mekong Subregion

The cross-border cooperation between Indonesia, Malaysia, and Singapore is notably distinct due to the sensitivity of their political systems to regional issues and the substantial natural, human, financial, and other resources at their disposal. Even during the era of President Suharto's strictly authoritarian regime, the Indonesian government made efforts to enhance cooperation with its wealthier neighbors. In 1967, the Malaysia–Indonesia General Border Committee (GBC) was established, initially focusing on security issues but expanding its agenda to include economic cooperation in 1984. In 1985, the Sosek-Malindo Working Committee was created, with a more pronounced focus on regional and socio-economic matters, such as trade, mobility, and infrastructure development (Karim 2015). In 1978, Indonesian authorities announced the creation of the Batam Free Trade Zone to attract investments from nearby Singapore. This zone was transformed in 2006 into the Batam–Bintan–Karimun Free Trade Zone, expanding its territory and offering investors additional customs and tax incentives.

The format of Indonesia's cross-border cooperation underwent significant changes following the resignation of authoritarian President Suharto in 1998. This political shift was accompanied by the decentralization of the country's political system and a substantial increase in the authority of regional governments, including in international relations. However, agreements signed by the regions still require central government approval, creating a degree of uncertainty and, in some cases, tensions between regional and central authorities. To circumvent legal restrictions, regional authorities sometimes rely on informal connections with the commercial sector, leveraging their licensing powers to foster such relationships. These dynamics have given rise to patron–client networks that regional governments use to advance their external economic interests (Karim et al. 2024).

Overall, the shift in the balance of power toward Indonesian regions has significantly boosted cross-border activities, stimulating cooperation in areas such as manufacturing, trade, infrastructure development, healthcare, education, and social welfare (Satyawan 2018).

Cross-border cooperation, however, remains heavily shaped by economic disparities, often disadvantaging Indonesia. The existence of the Batam free trade zone, for instance, is reliant on Singaporean investments, which has led to intense competition between the central government and local elites for control over financial flows (Karim 2019). In a different context, the Malaysian region of Sarawak is significantly more developed compared to Indonesia's West Kalimantan. Malaysia dominates the supply of goods to West Kalimantan, exploits Indonesian natural resources (such as palm oil production) and human resources (cheap labor), and often dictates the terms of joint projects, occasionally revising established agreements.

Additionally, a major challenge to Malaysian–Indonesian cooperation lies in the underdeveloped legal framework. For example, the Border Trade Agreement, signed in 1970, has not been updated to reflect the drastically changed realities of today (Elyta and Sahide 2021). Without significant modernization of such agreements, the potential for further enhancing cross-border collaboration remains limited, leaving much room for improvement in addressing these disparities.

2.6 Latin America

Latin American cross-border cooperation unfolds within complex political and economic contexts.

On the one hand, the predominance of Spanish-speaking countries in the region minimizes linguistic barriers, while cross-border interactions and projects are encouraged by regional integration organizations such as the Southern Common Market (MERCOSUR), the Andean Community (CAN), the Union of South American Nations (UNASUR), the Community of Latin American and Caribbean States

(CELAC), the Central American Integration System (SICA), and others. In some cases, cooperation is facilitated by the existence of twin border cities, such as Rivera (Uruguay) and Santana do Livramento (Brazil), Foz do Iguaçu (Brazil) and Ciudad del Este (Paraguay), and Táchira (Venezuela) and Cúcuta (Colombia). Similarly, geographic proximity enables collaboration between cities located slightly apart, as seen in the cross-border complex of Tacna (Peru) and Arica (Chile).

Brazil and Paraguay, in particular, are driven toward close cooperation by the joint management of the Itaipu Dam, the world's second-largest hydroelectric power plant. Operated by the binational company Itaipu Binacional, the dam employs tens of thousands of workers and provides over 70% of Paraguay's electricity and more than 15% of Brazil's electricity.

Yet, despite these favorable conditions, Latin American cross-border cooperation faces significant challenges that can undermine the positive factors and efforts mentioned earlier. Numerous political disagreements exist between Latin American states, and in some cases, between different levels of government within the same country. These disagreements, often exacerbated by territorial disputes, create an unfavorable backdrop for cooperation (Hurtado Bautista and Aponte Motta 2017; Dilla Alfonso and Contreras Vera 2021) (Fig. 2.6).

Fig. 2.6 Political map of Latin America

2.6 Latin America

Compared to the EU and North America, Latin American countries lack the extensive resources necessary to implement cross-border projects (Haarich 2018), such as grant programs to support cooperation, investments in cross-border infrastructure, or the promotion of transnational business initiatives. This shortfall is further exacerbated by the low levels of socio-economic development in many border regions and their challenging security environments.

Central governments typically dominate Latin American cross-border cooperation, often stifling local authorities' initiatives and limiting their powers (Dupeyron 2009). This situation is further compounded by the institutional weakness of local governments in some countries, such as Venezuela (Jimenez Aguilar and Thoene 2020). Additionally, typical issues in Latin American cross-border cooperation include the absence of binding legal commitments between parties (De Souza 2018), insufficient engagement of local border communities in joint projects (Dupeyron 2009), and relatively low levels of cross-border interaction among project participants, who often prefer to operate independently on their respective sides of the border (Barquet 2015).

As in the EU, cross-border cooperation in Latin America is actively promoted by regional integration organizations, which regard it as a tool for advancing integration, alleviating interstate tensions, and fostering the joint development of border areas and transnational connections. However, the activities of these organizations are often marked by instability (Malamud 2013; Kanai 2016), insufficient funding, and overlapping mandates. While such organizations sometimes establish bodies to coordinate cross-border cooperation, their effectiveness is frequently limited, with many becoming inactive just a few years after their creation (Wong Villanueva et al. 2023).

Within MERCOSUR, various aspects of cross-border cooperation fall under the purview of different bodies, working groups, and other institutions. Among these, the Council of the Common Market (which oversees the development and implementation of integration strategies) and the Trade Commission hold particular importance (Dupeyron 2009).

The Ad Hoc Group for Border Integration, established in 2002 at Brazil's initiative, operated under the authority of the Council of the Common Market. The group's objective was to formulate policies for the joint development of border regions and to enhance the effectiveness of cross-border cooperation. One of its achievements was the creation of rules ensuring access to medical services for border residents regardless of their nationality. However, the group's overall performance fell short of expectations, as it failed to reconcile national strategies for regional development and social policy effectively. Ultimately, these and other challenges led to the group's dissolution (De Souza 2016).

In 2008, the Working Group on Border Integration was established, aiming to incorporate the perspectives of local border authorities to a greater extent than its predecessor. The group also collaborated closely with the Structural Convergence Fund of MERCOSUR (FOCEM). Among other initiatives, the group took on the task of creating a database on border regions, addressing an issue that local authorities had struggled to manage effectively. However, over time, the group's activities were largely reduced to organizing discussion forums for local border authorities. In 2010, its work was suspended for five years, resuming in 2015 at the request of local authorities to discuss the ultimately unsuccessful idea of creating "Mercoregions" (i.e., MERCOSUR regions) (De Souza 2016). While the group remains active, its visibility in the public domain is rather limited.

The foremost mechanism for funding cross-border cooperation and other regional development initiatives within MERCOSUR is the MERCOSUR Structural Convergence Fund (FOCEM), established in 2005. The budget of this fund amounted to $100 million annually in the first decade of the 2000s (Amoroso Botelho 2014) and reached $300 million annually by 2022 (MERCOSUR 2021).

MERCOSUR actively seeks collaboration with international forums of regions and municipalities, such as the Forum of Consultative Municipalities, Federative States, Provinces, and Departments of MERCOSUR, as well as Mercociudades, involving them as advisors in shaping its cross-border cooperation policies. It is important to note that these institutions primarily serve as platforms for discussion and lack significant executive powers (Dupeyron 2009).

A notable contribution to the development of cross-border cooperation within MERCOSUR comes from the INNOVACT initiative, which aims to encourage innovation and foster collaboration at the local government level. In particular, it engages with the EU to transfer European cross-border cooperation practices and adapt them to Latin American contexts (Haarich 2018). However, INNOVACT lacks a formal institutional status within MERCOSUR as well as stable funding.

The activities of the Andean Community (CAN) in supporting cross-border cooperation are less extensive and ambitious compared to other regional initiatives. Nevertheless, it has achieved modest but tangible successes in providing legal and organizational support for bilateral cross-border cooperation among its members.

One significant initiative aimed at facilitating legal cross-border movement, reducing waiting times, and mitigating the negative effects of bureaucratic border and customs procedures is the establishment of Bi-national Border Assistance Centers (CEBAF) by several CAN members, including Bolivia, Peru, and Ecuador. These centers, jointly managed by neighboring countries, provide integrated services to individuals crossing the border. This initiative was authorized by Decision 502 of the Andean Community, adopted in 2001, which seeks to promote the legal flow of people and goods, eliminate barriers and redundant functions of control agencies, and encourage the exchange of information and best practices among participants (Comunidad Andina 2001).

A key aspect of UNASUR's policy for supporting cross-border cooperation is its substantial funding for ambitious infrastructure projects. The largest source of financing for such projects in South America is the Initiative for the Integration of Regional Infrastructure in South America (IIRSA), established in 2000 with the backing of all countries in the region. Operating under the aegis of UNASUR's Council for Infrastructure and Planning (COSIPLAN) and supported by a permanent secretariat, IIRSA aims to promote the development of interconnected transport, energy, and communication infrastructure across the region. This initiative has enabled South American countries to partially synchronize their planning for cross-border infrastructure development and to coordinate joint support for these projects. The total financing provided through IIRSA is estimated in the impressive range of hundreds of billions of dollars (Tomassian 2015). Despite its tangible achievements, the initiative has periodically faced interstate disputes and has been criticized for occasionally proceeding without adequate environmental safeguards, as well as for exacerbating regional inequalities in development (Kanai 2016).

In Central America, projects related to cross-border cooperation are also carried out under the aegis of SICA. As early as 1987, the Coordination Center for the Prevention of Natural Disasters in Central America (CEPREDENAC) was established to facilitate information exchange and provide assistance at both national and regional levels, along with the Regional Committee on Water Resources (CRRH) (Guinea Barrientos et al. 2015). In 2001, the Mesoamerican Integration and Development Project (MIDP) was launched under SICA, channeling investments amounting to billions of dollars into education, healthcare, and environmental initiatives.

The Development Bank of Latin America, which operates with an independent status, provides relatively modest yet significant support to local border communities. In 2007–2008, the bank established the Integration and Border Cooperation Development Program (PADIF), followed by the Cross-Border Cooperation and Integration Fund (COPIF) to finance its projects, with a budget of just a few million dollars. Unlike the larger programs mentioned earlier, PADIF and COPIF focused their efforts more specifically on supporting localized projects aimed at developing infrastructure, delivering social services, and ensuring environmental sustainability specifically in borderland areas (Oddone and Rodríguez Vázquez 2015).

While acknowledging the importance of the projects and mechanisms initiated within Latin American integration organizations, it is important to note that the predominant format for cross-border cooperation in the region remains bilateral (and less frequently multilateral) intergovernmental initiatives. These are typically managed through joint commissions, working groups, border committees, regional associations, and similar bodies (Dupeyron 2009).

In 1986, the governments of Guatemala, Honduras, and El Salvador launched the El Trifinio Initiative, marking one of the earliest efforts in the region to jointly manage a 7500 km^2 area at the intersection of their borders, encompassing biosphere reserves and protected natural areas. The initiative aimed to promote joint management of natural resources and improve living conditions for local populations. The lead role was taken by the Trilateral Commission, headed by senior officials from the central governments of the three countries, with local authorities playing a secondary role within the commission. This commission included a secretariat and specialized committees. While the project achieved notable successes in sustainable water resource management and biodiversity conservation, its efforts to address poverty and other socio-economic challenges yielded more modest results. Moreover, much of the implementation focused on activities within each country's borders, with limited transboundary engagement (Dilla Alfonso and Contreras Vera 2021).

In the 1990s, Joint Committees for the Integration and Development of Borders (CIDF) began to form in various border regions, including those between Argentina,

Bolivia, Brazil, Peru, Chile, and Ecuador. These committees coordinate cross-border interactions between governmental and non-governmental entities, address challenges related to cross-border mobility, promote the development of border areas, and draft relevant legislative proposals. To support these efforts, the committees can draw on development funds, which typically manage budgets in the range of several million dollars. However, the effectiveness of these funds is often hindered by bureaucratic challenges and limited financial resources (Dilla Alfonso and Contreras Vera 2021).

In 1996, the security forces of Argentina, Brazil, and Paraguay established the Joint Security Command. Its jurisdiction encompassed the tri-border area, a region known for its heightened criminal activity. The participating countries agreed to exchange information, conduct joint operations, and implement measures to safeguard tourism. This collaborative framework has remained relatively effective and continues to operate to this day (Manero 2007).

In 1998, as part of the peace agreement signed following the 1995 armed conflict, Ecuador and Peru established the Binational Fund for Peace and Development (FBPD) to foster peace and promote development in the regions adjacent to their shared border. The FBPD was launched with an initial capital of $300 million and is supported by the governments of both countries as well as international financial institutions such as the World Bank and the Inter-American Development Bank. The fund finances projects in various sectors, including infrastructure (construction of roads and bridges, improvement of water supply and sanitation systems, etc.), healthcare, education, agriculture, environmental protection, and the integration of border regions between the two nations (Rhi-Sausi and Oddone 2012).

In 2001, Bolivia, Chile, and Peru launched the "Aymara Without Borders Strategic Alliance," a project aimed at improving the living conditions of the transboundary Aymara people. While the initiative achieved limited success, it contributed to strengthening the cultural identity of the Aymara people and promoting cross-border cooperation. However, by 2015, the project had effectively lost its cross-border status due to disagreements among the participating countries (Dilla Alfonso and Contreras Vera 2021).

In 2002, two major initiatives were introduced to promote cross-border cooperation: one involving MERCOSUR members Brazil and Uruguay, and the other focusing on Andean Community members Peru and Colombia.

Under the Brazil-Uruguay "New Agenda for Border Cooperation and Development," various measures were outlined to enhance cross-border trade zones, develop transboundary infrastructure, significantly ease border crossing conditions for residents of certain border areas, increase mobility for educational and cultural exchange participants, implement shared access to healthcare and joint social programs, combat cross-border crime, promote transboundary tourism, engage in environmental cooperation, and manage emergencies collaboratively. Working groups composed of representatives from central and local authorities were established to address these issues.

As part of the "New Agenda," an integration zone was created between the twin cities of Rivera (Uruguay) and Santana do Livramento (Brazil), allowing residents to cross the border without undergoing customs procedures. For another pair of twin cities, both named Aceguá, a joint water supply and sanitation system was established. Several bridges over transboundary rivers were also constructed or upgraded (Dupeyron 2009).

Overall, the program can be considered relatively successful. However, its implementation has been hindered by challenges such as insufficient funding, the dominance of central authorities in project management, limited active participation of local communities, administrative barriers, and political disagreements between the parties (De Souza 2018).

Since 2002, the Border Integration Zone, aimed at fostering cross-border development in areas adjacent to the Peru-Colombia border, has been in operation. The zone was managed by a Bilateral Commission led by the foreign ministers of both countries and included representatives from central, regional, and local authorities. The day-to-day activities of the commission were overseen by an Executive Secretariat. In 2013, a Development Plan for the Border Integration Zone was adopted, followed by the establishment of a Bilateral Fund in 2015. Despite some progress in infrastructure development and relatively successful projects in agriculture, healthcare, and education, cooperation within the zone has lacked stability and sustainability (Hurtado Bautista and Aponte Motta 2017).

A distinctive form of cross-border cooperation in the region involves the establishment of transboundary protected areas, which focus on joint efforts to preserve biodiversity in regions spanning national borders. Funding for such initiatives from regional governments is typically limited. Therefore, considering the global importance of preserving regional biodiversity, securing financial support from international donors such as Conservation International, the World Bank, WWF, USAID, and others becomes a crucial factor for their success (Perrier Bruslé 2013).

One of the most extensive initiatives of this kind is the Mesoamerican Biological Corridor, established in the late 1990s. This corridor encompasses territories in Belize, Guatemala, Honduras, Costa Rica, Nicaragua, Panama, El Salvador, and parts of southern Mexican states. Another initiative with an even broader geographic and thematic scope, focusing on sustainable development and environmental conservation, is the Amazon Cooperation Treaty Organization (ACTO). Established in 1978 and given a permanent secretariat in 2002, ACTO includes seven regional countries (Manero 2007). Due to limited domestic resources, ACTO also actively seeks financial support from international donors.

The autonomous CBC powers of regions and cities are generally limited. However, regional authorities actively participate in planning and implementing regional development programs, engaging in bilateral border committees, and collaborating on cooperative projects with neighboring counterparts (Rhi-Sausi and Oddone 2012; Hurtado Bautista and Aponte Motta 2017). As noted earlier, certain regional organizations, particularly MERCOSUR, have taken steps toward encouraging central governments to grant their border regions and cities somewhat broader authority in shaping the agenda for interaction with foreign partners.

An example of relatively systematic cooperation between border cities can be seen in the Tacna–Arica urban complex. This partnership includes joint initiatives in infrastructure and transport development, trade promotion, and migration regulation (dating back to the 1950s) between the Peruvian city of Tacna and the Chilean city of Arica, located 56 km apart. Together, these cities have a combined population of over 500,000 and witness several million annual border crossings on the stretch between them. The interaction between these cities is multifaceted: Tacna residents often find employment in the more affluent Arica, and local businesses rely on the Arica port for maritime access. Meanwhile, Arica residents frequently visit Tacna for leisure and shopping (Dilla et al. 2022).

To advance cooperation in these areas—along with tourism, cross-border access to healthcare and education services, and combating smuggling and other transnational crimes—the two sides rely on existing intergovernmental agreements and work through bilateral integration committees to address ongoing issues. Key entities include the Arica-Tacna Regional Development Committee, which oversees economic and social matters, and the Bilateral Border Issues Commission, which focuses on border traffic regulation and crime prevention. While targeted joint efforts have achieved some success in infrastructure development and addressing social challenges, the complex's growth appears to be driven more by organic trends in trade and labor migration than by the coordinated actions of the two sides.

In 2005, the two largest countries in the region—Argentina and Brazil—signed the Agreement on Border Municipalities, which was only ratified in 2016. The agreement aimed to strengthen multifaceted ties between nine border cities in both countries, focusing on economic development, cross-border mobility regulation, employment arrangements, and access to healthcare and education services (República Argentina y República Federativa de Brasil 2009). While the agreement has achieved some success, further progress has been hindered, as in many similar cases, by persistent bureaucratic obstacles and political disagreements between the nations.

Non-governmental organizations have even less influence over key decision-making processes than border regions and cities. Nevertheless, they play an important—and in some cases, pivotal—role in Latin American cross-border cooperation. NGOs are often the driving force behind project initiatives, representing the interests of border populations, including indigenous communities, and securing funding from international donors.

NGOs have been particularly active in environmental protection. For instance, in 1999, government institutions, NGOs, scientists, indigenous community representatives, and other citizens from Bolivia, Brazil, and Peru launched the MAP Initiative (Madre de Dios–Acre–Pando). Developed by researchers, this initiative aimed to promote transboundary environmental conservation and mitigate the impacts of deforestation, the development of transport corridors, water resource exploitation, and urban growth in the tri-border region (Perrier Bruslé 2013; Wong Villanueva et al. 2023). In Central America, NGOs played a leading role in the aforementioned projects to establish transboundary protected areas (bioregions), implemented in collaboration with governments and international organizations (Barquet 2015).

2.7 Africa

Africa presents highly diverse conditions for the development of cross-border cooperation, shaped by its varied landscapes, ethnocultural and linguistic characteristics, levels of economic development, and political contexts (Fig. 2.7).

In many cases, cross-border cooperation in Africa is hindered by a combination of unfavorable conditions. One of the most significant is the artificial nature of most borders in the region, which were drawn by colonial powers without regard for long-standing economic and sociocultural ties between border communities. Many of these borders remain undemarcated to this day. Unsurprisingly, such boundaries are often perceived as artificial and disregarded by border communities that strive to maintain their traditional connections. At the same time, African states aim to pursue nation-building projects, assert control over borders, regulate cross-border movements, tax

Fig. 2.7 Africa

cross-border trade, and curb dangerous cross-border activities such as the movement of terrorist groups, human trafficking, arms smuggling, and poaching. Given that transboundary epidemics and epizootics pose greater risks in Africa than in most other regions, states also periodically attempt to use border controls as a barrier against health and sanitary threats. However, states often lack the capacity to ensure effective control over border regions. Their efforts are frequently met with resistance from border communities, which, in some cases, seek to establish an ordered alternative to that of the state, develop smuggling routes to bypass checkpoints, or form informal arrangements with border officials to circumvent restrictions (European Union 2015).

The dilemma between strengthening border security and fostering cross-border cooperation is further exacerbated by the limited resources available to African states. Collaborating countries in Africa typically lack substantial funds to implement joint projects, and the continent's generally underdeveloped transportation infrastructure hinders effective cross-border communication.

Several factors, however, actively support the development of cross-border cooperation in the region, sometimes granting it even greater dynamism than in other parts of the world.

First, the strong inclination of local communities to maintain close cross-border ties cannot be ignored by African states, which often aim to channel grassroots border activities into constructive and legal frameworks.

Second, the limited resources available to neighboring countries frequently drive them to cooperate by pooling resources and optimizing their joint use. This necessity is reflected in the presence of roughly a dozen major regional integration organizations, as well as the overarching African Union, which includes all African states.

Third, at least some African countries are more open than their counterparts in other regions to engaging with external actors, drawing on their expertise in cross-border cooperation, supported by donor funding and advisory assistance. Unlike most nations in Asia and Latin America, certain African states, such as Nigeria, Kenya, and Senegal, are willing to endorse the international engagement of their border regions, making them more receptive to the experiences of European CBC.

The European Union plays a particularly significant yet nuanced role in shaping African cross-border cooperation. On one hand, the EU aims to maintain and strengthen its position in the region as a leading actor wielding considerable soft power, with its governance model, including cross-border cooperation practices, presented as exemplary. In line with this strategy, the EU provides diverse forms of direct and indirect support to the region, including financial aid, trade preferences, and technical expertise. Programs and funds such as the European Fund for Sustainable Development and the Global Europe Programme, along with agreements like the 2000 Cotonou Agreement and the 2020 New EU–ACP Partnership Agreement, play a critical role in supporting African development initiatives, including cross-border projects, while also promoting trade. Unsurprisingly, the EU and its member states (notably Germany) collectively rank as the largest donors and co-organizers of African cross-border cooperation initiatives.

2.7 Africa

On the other hand, the EU's influence and promotion of its political priorities can distort the agenda for cross-border cooperation in the African region. The emphasis on boosting trade between the EU and Africa, for instance, often undermines intracontinental trade flows, weakens incentives for regional integration and cross-border collaboration, and contributes to disproportionate development in sectors of the economy oriented toward transcontinental exports. Additionally, the EU's policy of externalizing border security shifts responsibilities for combating irregular migration and terrorism onto source and transit countries. This approach is evident in initiatives like the 2015 Joint Valletta Action Plan, which focuses on European–African cooperation to combat illegal migration (European Union 2015), as well as agreements with Libya and West African countries on migration. While such policies aim to curb the growth of terrorist groups, human trafficking, and arms smuggling, they also exert significant pressure on African states, leading to stricter border controls and the implementation of measures that restrict mobility.

Conceptualizing African cross-border cooperation highlights the particular importance of informal cross-border trade, which typically centers on agricultural products. Many residents of border regions involved in such trade lack the necessary documents for crossing borders, as obtaining them is burdensome and costly. Another distinctive feature of informal cross-border trade is the predominance of women traders, who, in certain areas, account for 70–80% of participants. This makes them particularly vulnerable to violence and extortion by border officials and criminal elements (International Organization for Migration 2020). The weak control over informal traders crossing borders can also be exploited by transnational criminals, including terrorists, human traffickers, and arms smugglers.

The role of informal cross-border trade is perceived ambivalently by central and local authorities. On one hand, such trade provides employment opportunities for the growing population in border regions and enhances food security in these areas (Ahmodu-Tijani and Dosunmu 2020). On the other hand, it deprives governments of tax revenues, places tax-paying local businesses at a disadvantage (Ogalo 2010), and undermines the credibility of governmental efforts to tighten border controls aimed at combating serious transnational crimes (Iwata 2016).

Some researchers criticize African governments and international development programs for overlooking informal cross-border trade as a significant factor in the development of border regions (Ogalo 2010). In certain cases, authorities have made efforts to regulate and organize cross-border trade; yet, these efforts have often yielded mixed outcomes (Little et al. 2015).

In recent years, particularly systematic efforts have been made by three African regional integration organizations: COMESA (Common Market for Eastern and Southern Africa), EAC (East African Community), and SADC (Southern African Development Community). As early as 2008, COMESA introduced the Green Pass System, a health certification designed to formalize and facilitate the cross-border movement of livestock within the region (Little et al. 2015).

In 2018, COMESA, EAC, and SADC launched the Small-Scale Cross-Border Trade Initiative (SSCBTI) with financial support from the European Development Fund (€15 million). This program, implemented at selected border points between

Zambia and Zimbabwe, Tanzania, the Democratic Republic of Congo, Malawi, and Ethiopia with Kenya, aimed to facilitate small-scale cross-border trade, including reducing transaction costs and protecting traders from corruption and harassment. It introduced measures to enhance simplified trade regimes, such as reduced tariffs and streamlined customs procedures for goods below a specified value threshold originating from member states. Trade information desks were established near checkpoints to provide guidance, while capacity-building programs were launched to educate small-scale traders on trade regulations, market opportunities, and business skills. The program also included efforts to improve border infrastructure. The initiative was administered by the COMESA Secretariat, with organizational and technical support from the International Organization for Migration (IOM) and the International Trade Centre (ITC). Although initially scheduled to conclude in May 2022, the program was extended until the end of 2024 (Chibomba 2022).

Several African cross-border cooperation development programs exhibit a distinctly formalized, top-down character. These programs are often implemented with extensive international support and, in most cases, draw inspiration from the EU's model of cross-border cooperation. However, due to the lack of comparable financial resources and significant differences between European and African political and economic contexts, this model could not be fully replicated in the African setting.

Acting as the overarching continental organization, the African Union (AU) has sought to present a strategic agenda for cross-border cooperation across African nations, even though certain elements of this agenda appeared to align with the interests of only a subset of countries on the continent. In 2007, the AU adopted its Border Programme, which addressed both security and cooperation issues. Among other objectives, this program established principles for cross-border cooperation to guide African states in their collaborative efforts.

In 2014, the African Union adopted the Convention on Cross-Border Cooperation, which outlined forms and areas of collaboration, emphasized the key role of local authorities (Article 8) and subregional integration organizations (Article 9), and recommended the establishment of Border Consultative Committees for dialogue, problem diagnosis, and coordination of CBC, although it did not specify their composition. The Convention allowed for international agreements between local authorities of neighboring countries, provided they comply with national legislation. However, while it identified authorities at various levels as key actors in CBC, it made scant reference to non-state actors (African Union 2014). To date, the Convention has not entered into force, having been ratified by only eight ECOWAS member states.

In 2020, the AU adopted its Strategy for a Better Integrated Border Governance, which identified five key pillars: the development of capabilities for border governance; conflict prevention and resolution; border security and addressing transnational threats; mobility, migration, and trade facilitation; cooperative border management; and borderland development and community engagement. The primary actors responsible for implementing this strategy were designated as the AU itself, Regional

Economic Communities (RECs), and individual states (African Union Commission 2020).

Among the subregional organizations or Regional Economic Communities (RECs), the Economic Community of West African States (ECOWAS) stands out as one of the leading trendsetters in CBC on the continent. Its experience significantly influences the agenda promoted for the entire continent by the African Union. Several factors favor CBC within ECOWAS, including the use of a common currency—the West African CFA franc, operational in 8 of its 15 member states—and the 1979 ECOWAS Free Movement Protocols. These protocols grant citizens of member states the right to entry and residency, including visa-free movement between member countries for up to 90 days. This agreement has notably facilitated cross-border trade and seasonal transboundary pastoralism. However, the practical implementation of these protocols is hampered by diverging member state interests, particularly regarding security concerns. Moreover, the European Union (EU) has expressed apprehensions that the protocols may inadvertently facilitate terrorist activities and irregular migration networks. As a result, some member states periodically violate the agreement (Zanker et al. 2020).

In 2006, ECOWAS launched its ECOWAS Cross-Border Cooperation Programme, emphasizing the critical role of CBC in regional integration. Following an extended pilot phase that covered four regions, ECOWAS decided to roll out the ECOWAS CBC across all member states. This program, partially modeled after Interreg, featured a notably smaller budget, greater centralization in fund allocation, and less transparent mechanisms for implementation oversight.

The first phase of the program, running from 2017 to 2021, prioritized establishing joint border control points, developing border markets and trade hubs, supporting schools and border health centers, providing access to drinking water sources, and promoting social and economic development projects in border areas. The program's budget, supported by ECOWAS and international partners, totaled approximately $80 million, with $45.6 million allocated to project support, $19.2 million for capacity-building and awareness-raising activities, and $6.4 million for the support of networks and institutions (Jawara-N'Jai 2018). To coordinate project implementation in member states, National Platforms were established. In 2021, ECOWAS member state leaders approved a new program cycle, extending project support through 2025 (ECOWAS 2021).

Among the binational bodies specifically dedicated to CBC within the territorial framework of ECOWAS, the Nigeria–Niger Joint Commission for Cooperation (NNJCC) stands out. The NNJCC facilitates the implementation of economic and social projects in border areas, including the management of border trade, the development of telecommunications networks and transportation infrastructure, and the prevention of transboundary spread of diseases among humans and livestock (Zanker et al. 2020). The Commission's effectiveness has been limited, largely due to its inability to secure substantial funding for cooperation projects (Okechukwu 2018). The military coup in Niger in 2023, which led to the country's distancing from ECOWAS alongside Burkina Faso and Mali, casts serious doubt on the future effectiveness of the NNJCC.

Another subregional trendsetter in CBC is the East African Community (EAC). Its efforts to formalize informal cross-border trade have already been discussed. Additionally, the EAC has been among the key initiators in Africa of the One-Stop Border Post (OSBP) format, which enables border crossers to undergo migration and customs checks only once rather than twice. The establishment and development of OSBPs have been actively supported by international donors, including the World Bank, the EU, and individual countries (Nugent and Soi 2020). The EAC is also making strides in accelerating the adoption of electronic customs control technologies.

An atypical format of cooperation for the continent is the growth triangle established in 1999 between Zambia, Malawi, and Mozambique, inspired more by Southeast Asian experiences than European ones. The participants launched a series of projects aimed at pooling their mineral, logistical, and agricultural resources to enhance infrastructure, develop transport corridors, and promote joint ventures in agriculture, mining, and energy. The initiative received substantial financial backing from external sources, including a $100 million loan provided by the United Nations Development Programme for private-sector investments (Nshimbi 2015).

An important domain of CBC in Africa is the collaboration on border security issues. The most common forms of cooperation include the exchange of information and best practices among relevant security agencies. In certain cases, border guard services of neighboring countries establish Border Liaison Offices (BLOs) and joint task forces, such as the Multinational Joint Task Force in the Lake Chad Basin region, initiated by the African Union to combat the terrorist group Boko Haram (Nugent and Soi 2020). In many instances, cross-border security cooperation is supported by the AU, the EU, ECOWAS, and other international actors concerned with issues such as irregular migration, terrorism, and hazardous smuggling. However, such cooperation often falls short of achieving its goals due to political disagreements among participating countries.

Several influential intergovernmental organizations focused on environmental protection operate in Africa, often relying on external financial and organizational support. One of the oldest regional bodies of this kind is the Lake Chad Basin Commission, established in 1964 to regulate water use and develop other resources in the basin, as well as to address complaints and resolve international disputes related to these issues. The organization comprises six member states: Cameroon, Libya, Niger, Nigeria, Chad, and the Central African Republic. However, the Commission's effectiveness is limited due to disagreements among member states and inconsistent contributions to its approximately $1 million annual budget. Significant organizational and technical assistance is provided by international partners, including German institutions such as German Technical Cooperation. In contrast, the Lake Victoria Basin Commission, established in 2001 under the EAC framework, benefits from more substantial institutional and financial support. With a budget in the tens of millions of dollars—mostly funded by Germany and the EU, alongside contributions from member states—it operates more effectively and with a broader scope. Its activities include biodiversity conservation, which is facilitated by the absence of significant conflicts among the riparian countries (Scheumann and Herrfahrdt-Pähle 2008).

Transboundary NGO activism in Africa is generally confined to local scales due to the limited financial resources of its participants. However, in some instances, activists have managed to overcome these local boundaries by leveraging modern network communication technologies. A notable example is the Southern African Cross Borders Traders Association (SACBTA), established to protect the interests of informal entrepreneurs from ten Southern African countries, which now includes tens of thousands of members. The association provides its members with legal assistance and informational support to facilitate networking and cross-border engagement.

2.8 Russia

Russia has the second-longest land border in the world, matching China's number of UN-recognized neighboring states (14), plus two additional polities, Abkhazia and South Ossetia, whose independence is recognized by Russia but not by the vast majority of other states. The economic, political, and cultural diversity of states and regions bordering Russia likely surpasses that of China's neighbors. This diversity was reflected in the significant variations in Russia's CBC policies across different borders, which, until 2022, were heavily influenced by the European model of CBC in the west and have continued to be significantly shaped by the Chinese model in the east. Additionally, in the 1990s, discussions took place about establishing an ASEAN-style growth triangle in the Russian Far East involving Russian, Chinese, and North Korean territories, though this idea never materialized (Tsuji 2004). Russia's CBC with the unrecognized states of Abkhazia and South Ossetia also had its own distinct features, somewhat resembling the Chinese approach. To facilitate cooperation, the central government granted special powers to the bordering regions—Krasnodar Krai and the Republic of North Ossetia, respectively (Golunov 2021).

The characteristics of Russia's CBC have been shaped primarily by shifting political and economic realities. For most of the Soviet era, particularly from the 1930s until the late 1980s, cross-border mobility was heavily restricted and minimized. After the dissolution of the USSR and Russia's emergence as an independent state, the 1990s saw a dramatic weakening of central authority. This period brought several regions to the brink of declaring independence or semi-independence, granting themselves extensive powers. The new reality provided regions with broad opportunities to establish international ties almost autonomously, often in the context of a severe economic crisis. This crisis incentivized regions to seek their own revenue sources and encouraged the population to engage in cross-border shuttle trade.

Starting in the 2000s, the situation improved. Shuttle trade declined, and the central government, seeking to suppress separatism reminiscent of the 1990s and pursuing an increasingly authoritarian regime, significantly curtailed regions' powers in international activities. In practice, regional international engagement was largely reduced to lobbying for local enterprises and organizing ceremonial cultural events as part of official programs and visits.

In 2017, after more than a decade of discussion and revisions, the law "On the Basics of Cross-Border Cooperation" was adopted. It formally granted border regions and municipalities the right to conclude cooperation agreements with foreign partners of the same level. However, in practice, all such agreements still required approval from the central authorities (Russian Federation 2017). Despite these limitations, some regions—particularly those bordering China, increasingly seen as a strategic ally—took advantage of their formal rights to engage in CBC initiatives.

Under the central government's strict control over CBC, Russia's political leadership has placed significant emphasis on top-down regionalism as a political tool, particularly in the context of Eurasian integration and strengthening allied relations with China. As of late 2024, 20 Russia–Kazakhstan Interregional Cooperation Forums, 11 Russia–Belarus forums, and several multi-format Russia–China interregional forums had been held. These events, attended by top leadership from neighboring countries, regional governors, and representatives of major enterprises, were used to facilitate agreements between large regional players, initiate infrastructure projects, plan event programs, and shape the agenda for education and cultural initiatives.

Some infrastructure projects were closely tied to high-level politics, such as Russia–Kazakhstan transport infrastructure developments within China's Belt and Road Initiative (BRI). Another example is the North–South Corridor project, which gained heightened relevance after the sharp deterioration of relations between the EU and Russia following the Russia–Ukraine war in 2022. This corridor is intended to provide Russia with a convenient logistical link to Middle Eastern and South Asian markets.

Before 2022, Russia's CBC with neighboring EU countries (Finland, and from 2004, Estonia, Latvia, Lithuania, and Poland) was primarily influenced by the EU model. In the 1990s and 2000s, it was envisioned that Russia's CBC with its European partners would occur within a framework of regionalization, where Russian regions would gain autonomy comparable to that of their European counterparts (Baxendale et al. 2000). Russia indeed participated in the creation of several Euroregions, not only along its borders with the EU but also on the Russia–Ukraine border (Zhurzhenko 2004). Even the Russian–Kazakh–Mongolian–Chinese initiative Greater Altai in the early 2000s was presented by the Russian side as a Euroregion (Startsev 2016). However, most Russian Euroregions existed largely on paper. Even the relatively functional Russia–Finland Euroregion Karelia operated mostly as a mechanism for lobbying shared regional interests with central authorities (Rustamova 2019). Meanwhile, despite promoting rhetoric about border softening, the EU was reluctant to take decisive steps toward removing the rigid border, notably stalling negotiations on visa-free travel.

After Russia insisted on a special framework for its cooperation with the EU in the 2000s, the two sides reshaped their CBC in 2009. This restructuring effectively removed the element of cross-border regionalism while reinforcing another key component of the EU model—generous competitive funding for projects of various scales, ranging from local initiatives to cross-border infrastructure development. The EU and Russia launched several joint programs to support such projects, with the majority (some 70%) financed through the European Neighbourhood Initiative and the remainder covered by the Russian government (European External Action Service 2018). Following the outbreak of war in 2022, the EU ceased further funding for these programs, and EU countries bordering Russia imposed significantly stricter cross-border regulations.

Russia's CBC with Belarus and Kazakhstan is characterized by top–down instrumental regionalism. Both Belarus and Kazakhstan are members of the Eurasian Economic Union, and their CBC with Russia is facilitated by the absence of permanent customs controls at their borders. However, temporary customs checks and surrogate measures, such as food and transportation controls, are occasionally introduced during periods of heightened crises or disagreements (Golunov 2015).

In both cases, CBC primarily develops through industrial and trade connections between large and medium-sized enterprises, as well as small private businesses engaged in cross-border transportation. Nevertheless, differences between Russian–Belarusian and Russian–Kazakh CBC emerge due to distinct structural factors. On one hand, Belarus's more centralized political system results in relatively passive involvement of Belarusian regions, though the absence of regular migration controls and better transport proximity facilitates cooperation. On the other hand, Kazakh regions exhibit somewhat greater autonomy, but migration controls at the border significantly slow cross-border flows, and regional centers on either side of the border are typically much farther apart (often several hundred kilometers), which poses additional obstacles.

Russian–Chinese CBC has been somewhat more dynamic, driven by a range of factors. The disparity in economic structures plays a significant role, with Russia primarily exporting raw materials to China while importing finished industrial goods. Cultural contrasts also attract mutual interest: for Chinese tourists, Russia has long been the most affordable destination offering a European cultural experience, while Russian tourists are drawn to China's distinctively Asian culture. Additionally, the geographic and transport proximity of certain major cross-border population centers, such as the twin cities of Blagoveshchensk and Heihe, along with smaller town pairs, facilitates interaction. In the 1990s and 2000s, the relatively higher standard of living on the Russian side further encouraged engagement.

Another key factor has been China's proactive and strategic CBC policy, which has regarded ties with Russian regions as a crucial means of advancing the development of its northern provinces. For its part, Russia's declared "pivot to the East" in 2014, amid escalating tensions with the West, underscored its intention to prioritize relations with China, including programs aimed at fostering the development of its Far Eastern regions bordering the country.

Under significant, though not exclusive, influence from the Chinese experience, starting in the 1990s, Russian authorities periodically attempted to establish free economic zones (and in the 2010s, Priority Development Areas and free ports), both along the Chinese border and in other regions. These efforts, however, largely failed to achieve substantial success, as the zones were frequently exploited by entrepreneurs and regional authorities for customs fraud, tax evasion, and embezzlement of government funds. Additionally, overly centralized and sluggish bureaucratic systems deterred many foreign investors (Niyazbekova et al. 2019).

Overall, Russia–China CBC has achieved notable successes in increasing trade and promoting cross-border visits in areas with geographical and transport proximities. However, cooperation in cross-border planning and the development of transboundary transport infrastructure has been less successful, as project management on the Chinese side proved significantly more efficient than the Russian one. For instance, the Chinese side completed its portion of the railway bridge between Blagoveshchensk and Heihe in October 2018, whereas Russia only finished its segment in November 2019. Additionally, CBC is hindered by substantial cultural differences, the lack of a lingua franca, and trends toward equalizing living standards and prices in adjacent areas, which diminishes incentives for exploiting cross-border differences.

Nevertheless, given the near elimination of CBC between Russia and the EU after 2022, the Russia–China border remains the most promising area for CBC from Russia's perspective. In the post-Soviet period, following the opening of the border, cooperation with China became a vital factor in the economic development of Siberian and Far Eastern regions bordering China. It also helped to mitigate the alarmist sentiments that were relatively strong in the 1990s and 2000s in these regions, where part of the population feared the gradual annexation of these territories by China through alleged demographic and economic expansion (Alexseev 2012).

2.9 Conclusion

CBC across various regions of the world significantly varies in terms of conditions, starting positions of cooperating parties, priorities, scale, and achieved outcomes.

While the EU's experience is often regarded as a benchmark by both researchers and practitioners, it is largely unique due to characteristics such as its integration within a broader political and economic framework, the extensive autonomy granted to local authorities for implementing cross-border projects, the presence of robust legal mechanisms supporting cross-border organizations, and generous funding for competitive projects—encouraging diversity in the forms and areas of cooperation.

In other regions, CBC typically operates under conditions where local authorities have limited powers to foster cross-border interactions, and funding for such projects is modest. Under these constraints, CBC tends to have a narrower scope compared to the EU, focusing primarily on a limited set of priority areas.

However, this does not imply that CBC is strictly determined by specific regional local conditions. On the contrary, incorporating insights from the experiences of other regions, with careful consideration of regional and local conditions, can significantly broaden the range of available opportunities.

References

African Union. 2014. African Union convention on cross-border cooperation (Niamey Convention). https://www.peaceau.org/uploads/au-niamey-convention-eng.pdf.

African Union Commission. 2020. African Union strategy for a better integrated border governance. African Union Commission. https://archives.au.int/bitstream/handle/123456789/8851/African%20Union%20Strategy%20for%20a%20Better%20Integrated%20Border%20Governance.pdf?sequence=1&isAllowed=y.

Ahmodu-Tijani, Ismail Shola, and Kazeem Olanrewaju Dosunmu. 2020. Effects of the Informal Cross Border Trade in Western Africa: A Study of Nigeria and Niger. *Jurnal Aplikasi Manajemen, Ekonomi Dan Bisnis* 4 (2): 34–42.

Alexseev, Mikhail. 2012. The Chinese are coming: Public opinion and threat perception in the Russian Far East. 184. PONARS Eurasia Policy Memos. https://www.ponarseurasia.org/the-chinese-are-coming-public-opinion-and-threat-perception-in-the-russian-far-east/.

Amoroso Botelho, João Carlos. 2014. La Reducción de Las Asimetrías En MERCOSUR Como Una Forma de Ayuda al Desarrollo y de Cooperación Sur-Sur: El Caso Del FOCEM. *Geopolítica(s). Revista de Estudios Sobre Espacio y Poder* 4 (1): 43–62. https://doi.org/10.5209/rev_GEOP.2013.v4.n1.40538.

Anderson, James. 2008. Partition, consociation, border-crossing: Some lessons from the National Conflict in Ireland/Northern Ireland. *Nations and Nationalism* 14 (1): 85–104. https://doi.org/10.1111/j.1469-8129.2008.00340.x.

Anuar, Abdul Rahim, and Azhar Harun. 2018. Malaysia-Thailand cross border trade and cross border special economic zone potential: A case study of Rantau Panjang Sungai Kolok cross border town. *Journal of International Studies*.

Arieli, Tamar. 2016. Municipal cooperation across securitized borders in the post-conflict environment: The Gulf of Aqaba. *Territory, Politics, Governance* 4 (3): 319–336. https://doi.org/10.1080/21622671.2015.1042026.

ASEAN. 2021. ASEAN border management cooperation roadmap concept paper. https://asean.org/wp-content/uploads/2024/03/10.-Concept-Paper-ASEAN-Border-Management-Cooperation-Roadmap.pdf.

ASEAN. 2023. ASEAN launches new initiative to boost cross-border trade for MSMEs. *ASEAN*, November 23. https://asean.org/asean-launches-new-initiative-to-boost-cross-border-trade-for-msmes/.

Asher, Andrew D. 2012. Inventing a city: Cultural citizenship in 'Słubfurt.' *Social Identities* 18 (5): 497–520. https://doi.org/10.1080/13504630.2012.667601.

Balogh, Péter., and Márton. Pete. 2018. Bridging the gap: Cross-border integration in the Slovak-Hungarian Borderland around Štúrovo-Esztergom. *Journal of Borderlands Studies* 33 (4): 605–622. https://doi.org/10.1080/08865655.2017.1294495.

Barquet, Karina. 2015. Building a bioregion through transboundary conservation in Central America. *Norsk Geografisk Tidsskrift—Norwegian Journal of Geography* 69 (5): 265–276. https://doi.org/10.1080/00291951.2015.1087421.

Barrientos, Guinea, E. Héctor, Ashok Swain, Marcus B. Wallin, and Lars Nyberg. 2015. Disaster management cooperation in Central America: The case of rainfall-induced natural disasters. *Geografiska Annaler: Series A, Physical Geography* 97 (1): 85–96. https://doi.org/10.1111/geoa.12095.

Basboga, Kadir. 2022. A theme-based analysis of the intensity of cross-border cooperation across Europe. *Journal of Borderlands Studies* 37 (5): 955–973. https://doi.org/10.1080/08865655.2020.1833230.

Baxendale, James, Stephen Dewar, and David Gowan, eds. 2000. *The EU & Kaliningrad: Kaliningrad and the impact of EU enlargement*. London: Federal Trust.

BBC News. 2016. Kazakhstan's land reform protests explained. *BBC News*, April 28. https://www.bbc.com/news/world-asia-36163103.

Belt and Road Forum for International Cooperation. 2017. *Full text: Vision and actions on jointly building belt and road*. Belt and Road Forum for International Cooperation, April 10. http://2017.beltandroadforum.org/english/n100/2017/0410/c22-45.html.

Blatter, Joachim, and Norris Clement. 2000. II Introduction to the volume: Cross-border cooperation in Europe: Historical development, institutionalization, and contrasts with North America. *Journal of Borderlands Studies* 15 (1): 14–53. https://doi.org/10.1080/08865655.2000.9695541.

Boos, Greg, Greg McLawsen, and Heather Fathali. 2014. Canadian Indians, Inuit, Metis, and Metis: An exploration of the unparalleled rights enjoyed by American Indians born in Canada to freely access the United States. *Seattle Journal of Environmental Law*. https://digitalcommons.law.seattleu.edu/sjel/vol4/iss1/12.

Border Policy Research Institute. 2008. *Adapting the border to regional realities: Observations on exports at Buffalo and Blaine*. 39. Border Policy Research Institute Publications. https://cedar.wwu.edu/bpri_publications/39.

Border Policy Research Institute. 2011. *2011 Pacific Highway Southbound FAST lane study: Final report*. 90. Border Policy Research Institute Publications. https://cedar.wwu.edu/bpri_publications/90.

Border Policy Research Institute. 2013. *The wait-time system at the cascade gateway*. 17. Border Policy Research Institute Publications. https://cedar.wwu.edu/bpri_publications/17.

Border Policy Research Institute. 2014a. *2013/14 IMTC passenger vehicle survey: Project organization & report of findings*. 93. Border Policy Research Institute Publications. Border Policy Research Institute. https://cedar.wwu.edu/bpri_publications/93.

Border Policy Research Institute. 2014b. *Suggestions for improving cross-border mobility and North American competitiveness*. 94. Border Policy Research Institute Publications. Border Policy Research Institute. https://cedar.wwu.edu/bpri_publications/94.

Border Policy Research Institute. 2016. *Land-based freight flows between the US and Its NAFTA neighbors*. 6. Border Policy Research Institute Publications. https://cedar.wwu.edu/bpri_publications/6.

Border Policy Research Institute. 2017. *Modernizing the Columbia River Treaty*. 1. Border Policy Research Institute Publications. https://cedar.wwu.edu/bpri_publications/1.

Border Policy Research Institute. 2019. *Border barometer*. 112. Border Policy Research Institute Publications. https://cedar.wwu.edu/bpri_publications/112.

Border Policy Research Institute, and University of Buffalo Regional Institute. 2009. *Border barometer*. 99. Border Policy Research Institute Publications. https://cedar.wwu.edu/bpri_publications/99.

Bradley, John. 2018. The Irish-Northern Irish Economic Relationship: The Belfast Agreement, UK Devolution and the EU. *Ethnopolitics* 17 (3): 263–275. https://doi.org/10.1080/17449057.2018.1472423.

Broadhurst, Ginny, and Laurie Trautman. 2023. *Strengthening collaboration between Washington State and British Columbia*. 135. Border Policy Research Institute Publications. https://cedar.wwu.edu/bpri_publications/135.

Brooks, Tara, Lloyd Scott, John P. Spillane, and Katy Hayward. 2020. Irish construction cross border trade and Brexit: Practitioner perceptions on the periphery of Europe. *Construction Management and Economics* 38 (1): 71–90. https://doi.org/10.1080/01446193.2019.1679382.

Bruns, Bettina, and Judith Miggelbrink, eds. 2012. *Subverting borders: Doing research on smuggling and small-scale trade*. Wiesbaden: VS Verlag für Sozialwissenschaften.

Bruthiaux, Paul. 2008. Language education, economic development and participation in the Greater Mekong subregion. *International Journal of Bilingual Education and Bilingualism* 11 (2): 134–148. https://doi.org/10.2167/beb490.0.

Buchanan, Sandra. 2008. Transforming conflict in Northern Ireland and the border counties: Some lessons from the peace programmes on valuing participative democracy. *Irish Political Studies* 23 (3): 387–409. https://doi.org/10.1080/07907180802246719.

Bureau of Transportation Statistics. n.d. Tables & query tool. https://data.bts.gov/stories/s/Tables-Query-Tool/6rt4-smhh/. Accessed 20 Nov 2024.

References

Byrne, Sean, Olga Skarlato, Eyob Fissuh, and Cynthia Irvin. 2009. Building trust and goodwill in Northern Ireland and the border counties: The impact of economic aid on the peace process. *Irish Political Studies* 24 (3): 337–363. https://doi.org/10.1080/07907180903075801.

Caesar, Beate. 2017. European groupings of territorial cooperation: A means to harden spatially dispersed cooperation? *Regional Studies, Regional Science* 4 (1): 247–254. https://doi.org/10.1080/21681376.2017.1394216.

Cairncross, Frances. 1997. *The death of distance: How the communications revolution is changing our lives.* Cambridge, MA: Harvard Business Review Press.

Cairo, Heriberto, María Lois, Pedro Limón, Sergio Claudio González, and Joan Bauzà. 2024. Mapping with(out) borders: An exploratory cartography of cross-border cooperation in the Spanish-Portuguese Raya/Raia. *Journal of Maps* 20 (1): 2374337. https://doi.org/10.1080/17445647.2024.2374337.

Calzada, Igor. 2015. Benchmarking cross-border city-regions: Basque and Øresund comparative territorial connection. *Regions Magazine* 297 (1): 4–8. https://doi.org/10.1080/13673882.2015.11431633.

Capello, Roberta, Andrea Caragliu, and Ugo Fratesi. 2018. Breaking down the border: Physical, institutional and cultural obstacles. *Economic Geography* 94 (5): 485–513. https://doi.org/10.1080/00130095.2018.1444988.

Cappellano, Francesco. 2019. *Cross border innovation economies: The cascadia innovation corridor case.* 116. Border Policy Research Institute Publications. https://cedar.wwu.edu/bpri_publications/116.

Cappellano, Francesco, and Annalisa Rizzo. 2019. Economic drivers in cross-border regional innovation systems. *Regional Studies, Regional Science* 6 (1): 460–468. https://doi.org/10.1080/21681376.2019.1663256.

Cappellano, Francesco, and Teemu Makkonen. 2020. The proximity puzzle in cross-border regions. *Planning Practice & Research* 35 (3): 283–301. https://doi.org/10.1080/02697459.2020.1743921.

Cappellano, Francesco, Kathrine Richardson, and Laurie Trautman. 2021. Cross border regional planning: Insights from cascadia. *International Planning Studies* 26 (2): 182–197. https://doi.org/10.1080/13563475.2020.1779672.

Chibomba, Muzinge. 2022. Small-scale cross-border trade initiative extended by 31 months—Common Market for Eastern and Southern Africa (COMESA). *COMESA*, August 11. https://www.comesa.int/small-scale-cross-border-trade-initiative-extended-by-31-months/.

Christmann, Nathalie, Martine Mostert, Pierre-François. Wilmotte, Jean-Marc. Lambotte, and Mario Cools. 2020. Opportunities for reinforcing cross-border railway connections: The case of the Liège (Belgium)—Maastricht (the Netherlands) connection. *European Planning Studies* 28 (1): 105–124. https://doi.org/10.1080/09654313.2019.1623976.

Chu, Vivian H.Y., and Anna Ka-yin Lee. 2019. Institutional obstacles and opportunities for policy entrepreneurship in cross-border environmental management: A case study in China's Greater Pearl River Delta region. *Asian Geographer* 36 (2): 165–83. https://doi.org/10.1080/10225706.2018.1563797.

Church, Andrew, and Peter Reid. 1996. Urban power, international networks and competition: The example of cross-border cooperation. *Urban Studies* 33 (8): 1297–1318. https://doi.org/10.1080/0042098966664.

Clauson, Stacey, and Laurie Trautman. 2016. *Braided freshwater governance: A case study of regulation and stewardship of riparian areas and wetlands in British Columbia and Washington State.* 2. Border Policy Research Institute Publications. https://cedar.wwu.edu/bpri_rr/2.

Comunidad Andina. 2001. *DECISIÓN 502: Centros Binacionales de Atención Fronteriza (CEBAF) En La Comunidad Andina.* Secretaría General de la Comunidad Andina. https://www.comunidadandina.org/StaticFiles/DocOf/DEC502.pdf.

Conroy, Hugh. 2011. *Advancing U.S.–Canada border transportation planning and programming.* 76. Border Policy Research Institute. https://cedar.wwu.edu/bpri_publications/76.

Council of Europe. 1980. *European outline convention on transfrontier co-operation between territorial communities or authorities.* 106. European Treaty Series. Madrid. https://rm.coe.int/168 0078b0c.
Council of Europe. 1995. *Additional protocol to the European outline convention on transfrontier cooperation between territorial communities or authorities.* 159. European Treaty Series. Strasbourg. https://rm.coe.int/168007cdae.
Cressati, Claudio, Mauro Pascolini, and Daniel Spizzo. 2010. The Alpine—Adriatic—Danubian Euroregion: Geo-political and institutional issues. *disP—The Planning Review* 46 (183): 41–48. https://doi.org/10.1080/02513625.2010.10557110.
Davidson, David. 2014. *The Columbia River Treaty review: A synopsis.* 12. Border Policy Research Institute Publications. https://cedar.wwu.edu/bpri_publications/12.
Davies, Gemma. 2021. Facilitating cross-border criminal justice cooperation between the UK and Ireland After Brexit: 'Keeping the Lights On' to ensure the safety of the common travel area. *The Journal of Criminal Law* 85 (2): 77–97. https://doi.org/10.1177/0022018320977528.
De Fátima Amante, Maria. 2010. Local discursive strategies for the cultural construction of the border: The case of the Portuguese–Spanish border. *Journal of Borderlands Studies* 25 (1): 99–114. https://doi.org/10.1080/08865655.2010.9695754.
De Sousa, Luis. 2013. Understanding European cross-border cooperation: A framework for analysis. *Journal of European Integration* 35 (6): 669–687. https://doi.org/10.1080/07036337.2012.711827.
De Souza, Gustavo Matiuzzi. 2016. The Institutionalization process of border integration in Mercosur (2003–2015): Regional Uncoordinated attempts toward social development. *Fédéralisme Régionalisme.* https://popups.uliege.be/1374-3864/index.php?id=1654.
De Souza, Gustavo Matiuzzi. 2018. *Local perceptions on the new agenda for cooperation and border development in the Brazilian-Uruguayan cross-border region.* Porto Alegre, Brazil: Pontifical Catholic University of Rio Grande do Sul (PUCRS). https://www.escavador.com/sobre/377547 466/gustavo-matiuzzi-de-souza.
Decoville, Antoine, and Frédéric. Durand. 2016. Building a cross-border territorial strategy between four countries: Wishful thinking? *European Planning Studies* 24 (10): 1825–1843. https://doi.org/10.1080/09654313.2016.1195796.
Deiana, Maria-Adriana., Milena Komarova, and Cathal McCall. 2019. Cross-border cooperation as conflict transformation: Promises and limitations in EU peacebuilding. *Geopolitics* 24 (3): 529–540. https://doi.org/10.1080/14650045.2019.1599518.
Den Broek, Van, Roel Rutten Jos, and Paul Benneworth. 2020. Innovation and SMEs in interreg policy: Too early to move beyond bike lanes? *Policy Studies* 41 (1): 1–22. https://doi.org/10.1080/01442872.2018.1539225.
Dilla, Haroldo, Maria Fernanda Cabezas, and Margarita Tamara Figueroa. 2022. Notes for a discussion on Latin American cross-border regions. *Journal of Borderlands Studies* 37 (3): 435–451. https://doi.org/10.1080/08865655.2020.1784033.
Dilla Alfonso, Haroldo, and Camila Contreras Vera. 2021. Fronterización y Concertaciones Transfronterizas En América Latina. *Estudios Fronterizos* 22 (April). https://doi.org/10.21670/ref.2106069.
Dimitrov, Mitko, George Petrakos, Stoyan Totev, and Maria Tsiapa. 2003. Cross-border cooperation in Southeastern Europe. *Eastern European Economics* 41 (6): 5–25. https://doi.org/10.1080/001 28775.2003.11041063.
Dimitrovova, Bohdana. 2012. Imperial re-bordering of Europe: The case of the European neighbourhood policy. *Cambridge Review of International Affairs* 25 (2): 249–267. https://doi.org/10.1080/09557571.2012.678298.
Directive 2011/24/EU of the European Parliament and of the Council of 9 March 2011 on the application of patients' rights in cross-border healthcare. 2011. *OJ L.* Vol. 088. http://data.eur opa.eu/eli/dir/2011/24/oj/eng.
Dodder, Richard A., and Lubomir Faltan. 1998. Cross-border regional cooperation: Current concerns in Slovakia. *Nationalities Papers* 26 (2): 303–311. https://doi.org/10.1080/00905999808408565.

Domaniewski, Stanislaw, and Dominika Studzińska. 2016. The small border traffic zone between Poland and Kaliningrad region (Russia): The impact of a local visa-free border regime. *Geopolitics* 21 (3): 538–555. https://doi.org/10.1080/14650045.2016.1176916.

Dupeyron, Bruno. 2009. Regional integration and border interactions in the Cuenca Del Plata: Legacies, achievements and challenges for the Mercosur. *Journal of Borderlands Studies* 24 (3): 131–151. https://doi.org/10.1080/08865655.2009.9695744.

Dupeyron, Bruno. 2017. 'Secondary Foreign Policy' through the Prism of cross-border governance in the US–Canada Pacific Northwest border region. *Regional & Federal Studies* 27 (3): 321–340. https://doi.org/10.1080/13597566.2017.1343722.

Durand, Frédéric. 2014. Challenges of cross-border spatial planning in the metropolitan regions of Luxembourg and Lille. *Planning Practice & Research* 29 (2): 113–132. https://doi.org/10.1080/02697459.2014.896148.

ECOWAS. 2021. Mise En Œuvre Du Programme de Coopération Transfrontalière de La CEDEAO: Les Points Focaux Des Etats Membres Échangent Sur La Libre Circulation et Le Mécanisme de Financement Régional. | Economic Community of West African States (ECOWAS). ECOWAS. June 2. https://www.ecowas.int/mise-en-oeuvre-du-programme-de-cooperation-transfrontal iere-de-la-cedeao-les-points-focaux-des-etats-membres-echangent-sur-la-libre-circulation-et-le-mecanisme-de-financement-regional/?lang=fr.

Elyta, Elyta, and Ahmad Sahide. 2021. Model of creative industry management in border areas to improve bilateral cooperation in Indonesia and Malaysia. Edited by Richard Meissner. *Cogent Social Sciences* 7 (1): 1974670. https://doi.org/10.1080/23311886.2021.1974670.

Engl, Alice, and Estelle Evrard. 2020. Agenda-setting dynamics in the post-2020 cohesion policy reform: The pathway towards the European cross-border mechanism as possible policy change. *Journal of European Integration* 42 (7): 917–935. https://doi.org/10.1080/07036337.2019.1689969.

Environmental Cooperation Agreement between the Province of British Columbia and the State of Washington. 1992. https://www2.gov.bc.ca/assets/gov/environment/natural-resource-policy-legislation/environmental-policy/bcwaccord.pdf.

Eskelinen, Heikki, and Pirjo Jukarainen. 2000. New crossings at different borders: Finland. *Journal of Borderlands Studies* 15 (1): 255–279. https://doi.org/10.1080/08865655.2000.9695549.

European Commission. 2024. B-solutions: Solving border obstacles. European Commission Regional Policy. May 15. https://ec.europa.eu/regional_policy/whats-new/panorama/2024/05/15-05-2024-b-solutions-solving-border-obstacles_en.

European Commission. n.d. European Territorial Cooperation (Interreg). https://ec.europa.eu/regional_policy/policy/cooperation/european-territorial_en. Accessed 14 Nov 2024.

European External Action Service. 2018. EU-Russia Cross-Border Cooperation (CBC) Programs Overview. *European External Action Service* (blog). July 31. https://www.eeas.europa.eu/node/48999_en.

European Parliament. 2018. Proposal for a regulation on a mechanism to resolve legal and administrative obstacles in a cross-border context. | Legislative Train Schedule. European Parliament. 2018. https://www.europarl.europa.eu/legislative-train/spotlight-MFF/file-mff-mechanism-to-resolve-cross-border-obstacles.

European Union. 2015. *Valletta summit, 11–12 November 2015 action plan*. Valletta: Council of the European Union. https://www.consilium.europa.eu/media/21839/action_plan_en.pdf.

"EUSALP Territories: 7 countries and 48 regions—EUSALP." n.d. https://alpine-region.eu/about/territories. Accessed 21 Nov 2024.

Evrard, Estelle. 2016. The European Grouping of Territorial Cooperation (EGTC): Towards a supraregional scale of governance in the greater region SaarLorLux? *Geopolitics* 21 (3): 513–537. https://doi.org/10.1080/14650045.2015.1104667.

Faludi, Andreas. 2008. European territorial cooperation and learning: Reflections by the Guest Editor on the wider implications. *disP—The Planning Review* 44 (172): 3–10. https://doi.org/10.1080/02513625.2008.10556998.

Framework agreement on integrated cross-border Maritime law enforcement operations between the government of the United States of America and the Government of Canada. 2009. https://www.dhs.gov/xlibrary/assets/shiprider_agreement.pdf.

Framework for Co-Operation: Spatial Strategies of Northern Ireland & the Republic of Ireland. 2010. Dublin, Belfast: Department for Regional Development (Northern Ireland); Department of the Environment, Community and Local Government (Republic of Ireland). https://www.gov.ie/pdf/?file=/assets.gov.ie/111273/1a8242ae-85fe-4245-8d0a-aa353e92f81c.pdf.

Frank, Andrea I. 2013. Cohesion, coherence, cooperation: European Spatial planning coming of age? *International Planning Studies* 18 (2): 267–269. https://doi.org/10.1080/13563475.2012.734683.

Freelan, Stefan. n.d. "Salish Sea." *Stefan Freelan Cartography.* https://www.stefanfreelan.com/salishsea/.

Fricke, Carola. 2015. Spatial governance across borders revisited: Organizational forms and spatial planning in metropolitan cross-border regions. *European Planning Studies* 23 (5): 849–870. https://doi.org/10.1080/09654313.2014.887661.

Fritsch, Matti, Sarolta Németh, Minna Piipponen, and Gleb Yarovoy. 2015. Whose partnership? Regional participatory arrangements in CBC programming on the Finnish-Russian border. *European Planning Studies* 23 (12): 2582–2599. https://doi.org/10.1080/09654313.2015.1096916.

Future Borders Coalition. n.d. "Our Story." Future Borders Coalition. https://www.futurebordercoalition.org. Accessed 24 Nov 2024.

Gabbe, Jens. 2015. *European experiences of cross-border cooperation.* Choibalsan: Committee of Local Cooperation.

Gasparini, Alberto. 2014. Belonging and identity in the European border towns: Self-centered borders, Hetero-Centered Borders. *Journal of Borderlands Studies* 29 (2): 165–201. https://doi.org/10.1080/08865655.2014.916067.

Gkintidis, Dimitrios. 2013. Rephrasing nationalism: Elite representations of Greek-Turkish Relations in a Greek border region. *Southeast European and Black Sea Studies* 13 (3): 455–468. https://doi.org/10.1080/14683857.2013.824665.

Globerman, Steven, and Paul Storer. 2014. *An assessment of future bilateral trade flows and their implications for U.S. border infrastructure investment.* 68. Border Policy Research Institute Publications. https://cedar.wwu.edu/bpri_publications/68.

Golunov, Serghei. 2015. How Russia's Food Embargo and Ruble devaluation challenge the Eurasian customs union. 363. PONARS Eurasia Policy Memos. https://www.ponarseurasia.org/how-russia-s-food-embargo-and-ruble-devaluation-challenge-the-eurasian-customs-union/.

Golunov, Serghei. 2021. Cross-border cooperation of post-Soviet de facto states (in Russian). *Comparative Politics Russia.*

Gomez Prieto, J. 2016. Impact of European Territorial Cooperation (ETC) on the promotion and use of solar energy in the mediterranean. *Regional Studies, Regional Science* 3 (1): 185–192. https://doi.org/10.1080/21681376.2016.1150198.

Government of Canada, Canada Border Services Agency. 2019. Entry Exit Initiative—Final implementation – Executive Summary. May 2. https://www.cbsa-asfc.gc.ca/agency-agence/reports-rapports/pia-efvp/atip-aiprp/eei-ies-eng.html.

Great Lakes Fishery Commission. n.d. Great Lakes Fishery Commission—About. https://www.glfc.org/about.php. Accessed 25 Nov 2024.

Greater Mekong Subregion. n.d. "Overview of the Greater Mekong Subregion Economic Cooperation Program | Greater Mekong Subregion (GMS)." Greater Mekong Subregion. https://www.greatermekong.org/overview-greater-mekong-subregion-economic-cooperation-program. Accessed 25 Nov 2024.

Gubrium, Erika, Aadne Aasland, Benedikte V. Lindskog, Erika Arteaga, and Igor Mikheev. 2024. 'It Seemed Like Forever!' Shrinking Spaces of Conviviality at the Border of Norway and Russia. *Journal of Borderlands Studies*, January, 1–20. https://doi.org/10.1080/08865655.2024.2307608.

References

Haarich, Silke. 2018. Smart specialisation in peripheral and border regions in Latin America—Challenges and lessons. INNOVACT. https://www.regionalstudies.org/wp-content/uploads/2018/09/Haarich-INNOVACT_Seville-s3_26sep18.pdf.

Hale, Geoffrey. 2011. Politics, people and passports: Contesting security, travel and trade on the US-Canadian border. *Geopolitics* 16 (1): 27–69. https://doi.org/10.1080/14650045.2010.493768.

Hale, Geoffrey. 2019. Borders near and far: The economic, geographic and regulatory contexts for trade and border-related issues in landlocked Alberta. *Journal of Borderlands Studies* 34 (2): 157–180. https://doi.org/10.1080/08865655.2017.1315609.

Hansen, Christian Lorens. 2000. Economic, political, and cultural integration in an inner European Union border region: The Danish-German border region. *Journal of Borderlands Studies* 15 (2): 91–118. https://doi.org/10.1080/08865655.2000.9695558.

Hataley, Todd, and Christian Leuprecht. 2018. Determinants of cross-border cooperation. *Journal of Borderlands Studies* 33 (3): 317–328. https://doi.org/10.1080/08865655.2018.1482776.

Hayward, Katy. 2021. 'Flexible and imaginative': The EU's accommodation of Northern Ireland in the UK–EU withdrawal agreement. *International Studies* 58 (2): 201–218. https://doi.org/10.1177/00208817211001999.

Herzog, Lawrence A., and Christophe Sohn. 2019. The co-mingling of bordering dynamics in the San Diego-Tijuana cross-border metropolis. *Territory, Politics, Governance* 7 (2): 177–199. https://doi.org/10.1080/21622671.2017.1323003.

Hurtado Bautista, Adriana Mayela, and Jorge Aponte Motta. 2017.¿Hacia Un Gobierno Transfronterizo? Explorando La Institucionalidad Para La 'Integración' Colombo-Peruana. *Estudios Fronterizos* 18 (35): 70–89. https://doi.org/10.21670/ref.2017.35.a04.

IMTC. n.d. About The IMTC. https://theimtc.com/about/. Accessed 24 Nov 2024.

Inforegio—B Solutions: Solving Border Obstacles. n.d. https://ec.europa.eu/regional_policy/whats-new/panorama/2024/05/15-05-2024-b-solutions-solving-border-obstacles_en. Accessed 14 Nov 2024.

Institute of History, Archaeology and Ethnography of the Peoples of the Far East, Far-Eastern branch of RAS, and Sergey Pestsov. 2021. Cross-border cooperation of Russia and China: Chaotic prosperity and ordered degradation. *Vestnik of Saint Petersburg University. International relations* 14 (1): 20–40. https://doi.org/10.21638/spbu06.2021.102.

International Joint Commission. 2018. Air quality. International Joint Commission. July 18. https://www.ijc.org/en/what/air-quality.

International Organization for Migration. 2020. *Making the case to integrate human mobility into cross-border trade and trade facilitation*. Geneva, Switzerland: International Organization for Migration. https://www.comesa.int/wp-content/uploads/2020/09/Making-the-case-to-integrate-human-mobility_v06_11Aug2020b.pdf.

Iwata, Takuo. 2016. Borders and regional security in local governments' cooperation in West Africa: Case Studies in Burkina Faso 15: 1–25.

Jakubowski, Andrzej, Karolina Trykacz, Tomasz Studzieniecki, and Jakub Skibiński. 2022. Identifying cross-border functional areas: Conceptual background and empirical findings from Polish Borderlands. *European Planning Studies* 30 (12): 2433–2455. https://doi.org/10.1080/09654313.2021.1958760.

János, Dr Sallai, and Csaba Jónás. 2004. The Ukrainian-Hungarian border: Security and cross-border relations. *Global Crime* 6 (3–4): 387–390. https://doi.org/10.1080/17440570500277284.

Jauhiainen, Jussi. 2002. Territoriality and topocracy of cross-border networks. *Journal of Baltic Studies* 33 (2): 156–176. https://doi.org/10.1080/01629770200000031.

Jawara-N'Jai, Kinza. 2018. Presentation on the ECOWAS regional cross-border cooperation support programme (ERCBCSP): What legal and financial scenarios for cross-border activities? Presented at the Seminar on Cross-Border Development in the Sahel, Cotonou, Cotonou, Benin. https://www.slideshare.net/slideshow/presentation-on-the-ecowas-regional-crossborder-cooperation-support-programme-ercbcsp-what-legal-and-financial-scenarios-for-crossborder-activities/109205897.

Jimenez Aguilar, Carlos M., and Ulf Thoene. 2020. Frontier development policy and local governance in South America. *Territory, Politics, Governance* 8 (5): 639–656. https://doi.org/10.1080/21622671.2019.1612271.

Kaewkumkong, Ampa, and Ke Sen. 2019. Challenges of the buffer school policy implementation in the ASEAN community era: The case of the Thailand-Cambodia Border. *Asia Pacific Journal of Education* 39 (2): 237–251. https://doi.org/10.1080/02188791.2019.1621798.

Kanai, J. Miguel. 2016. The pervasiveness of neoliberal territorial design: Cross-border infrastructure planning in South America since the introduction of IIRSA. *Geoforum* 69 (February): 160–170. https://doi.org/10.1016/j.geoforum.2015.10.002.

Kang, Yuyang, and Jin Jiang. 2020. Revisiting the innovation systems of cross-border cities: The role of higher education institution and cross-boundary cooperation in Hong Kong and Shenzhen. *Journal of Higher Education Policy and Management* 42 (2): 213–229. https://doi.org/10.1080/1360080X.2019.1701849.

Karim, Moch Faisal. 2019. State transformation and cross-border regionalism in Indonesia's Periphery: Contesting the centre. *Third World Quarterly* 40 (8): 1554–1570. https://doi.org/10.1080/01436597.2019.1620598.

Karim, Moch Faisal, Tirta Nugraha Mursitama, Sayed Fauzan Riyadi, Roseno Aji Affandi, and Fairuz Muzdalifa. 2024. Informality, paradiplomacy, and cross-border cooperation: The development of tourism on Bintan Island, Indonesia. *Asian Studies Review* 48 (2): 370–388. https://doi.org/10.1080/10357823.2023.2259080.

Karim, Mochammad. 2015. Local-central dynamics and limitations of micro-regionalism: Understanding West Kalimantan and Sarawak Cross-Border Cooperation. In *Balanced growth for an inclusive and equitable ASEAN community*, edited by Mely Caballero-Anthony and Richard Barichello, 86–124. Singapore: S. Rajaratnam School of International Studies (RSIS), Nanyang Technological University.

Kashin, Vasily, and Alexandra Yankova. 2021. Cross-border cooperation between Russia and China: Overcoming deep obstacles. *SSRN Electronic Journal*. https://doi.org/10.2139/ssrn.3964667.

Khasson, Viktoriya. 2013. Cross-border cooperation over the Eastern EU Border: Between assistance and partnership under the European neighbourhood and partnership instrument. *East European Politics* 29 (3): 328–343. https://doi.org/10.1080/21599165.2013.807802.

Klatt, Martin. 2014. (Un)familiarity? Labor related cross-border mobility in Sønderjylland/Schleswig since Denmark joined the EC in 1973. *Journal of Borderlands Studies* 29 (3): 353–373. https://doi.org/10.1080/08865655.2014.938968.

Klatt, Martin, and Hayo Herrmann. 2011. Half empty or half full? Over 30 years of regional cross-border cooperation within the EU: Experiences at the Dutch-German and Danish-German border. *Journal of Borderlands Studies* 26 (1): 65–87. https://doi.org/10.1080/08865655.2011.590289.

Knippschild, Robert, and Thorsten Wiechmann. 2012. Supraregional partnerships in large cross-border areas—Towards a new category of space in Europe? *Planning Practice and Research* 27 (3): 297–314. https://doi.org/10.1080/02697459.2012.670933.

Koch, Katharina. 2015. Region-building and security: The multiple borders of the Baltic Sea Region after EU enlargement. *Geopolitics* 20 (3): 535–558. https://doi.org/10.1080/14650045.2015.1026964.

Koff, Harlan. 2015. Informal economies in European and American cross-border regions. *Journal of Borderlands Studies* 30 (4): 469–487. https://doi.org/10.1080/08865655.2016.1165133.

Kosonen, Riitta, Xu Feng, and Erja Kettunen. 2008. Paired border towns or TwinCities from Finland and China. *Chinese Journal of Population Resources and Environment* 6 (1): 3–13. https://doi.org/10.1080/10042857.2008.10684849.

Krainara, Choen, and Jayant K. Routray. 2015. Cross-border trades and commerce between Thailand and Neighboring countries: Policy implications for establishing special border economic zones. *Journal of Borderlands Studies* 30 (3): 345–363. https://doi.org/10.1080/08865655.2015.1068209.

References

Kramsch, Olivier. 2001. Navigating the spaces of Kantian reason: Notes on cosmopolitical governance within the cross-border *Euregios* of the European Union. *Geopolitics* 6 (2): 27–50. https://doi.org/10.1080/14650040108407716.

Kramsch, Olivier Thomas. 2003. The temporalit(Ies) of European cross-border governance: *Euregios* and the problem of Sens. *Journal of Borderlands Studies* 18 (2): 69–85. https://doi.org/10.1080/08865655.2003.9695607.

Laffan, Brigid, and Diane Payne. 2003. INTERREG III and cross-border cooperation in the Island of Ireland. *Perspectives on European Politics and Society* 4 (3): 447–473.

Lange, Emily. 2018. Cross-border cooperation in action: Taking a closer look at the Galicia-North of Portugal European Grouping of territorial cooperation. *Journal of Borderlands Studies* 33 (3): 415–431. https://doi.org/10.1080/08865655.2016.1195701.

Leuprecht, Christian, Todd Hataley, Kelly Sundberg, Keith Cozine, and Emmanuel Brunet-Jailly. 2021. The United States-Canada security community: A case study in mature border management. *Commonwealth & Comparative Politics* 59 (4): 376–398. https://doi.org/10.1080/14662043.2021.1994724.

Liberato, Dália., Elisa Alén, Pedro Liberato, and Trinidad Domínguez. 2018. Governance and cooperation in Euroregions: Border tourism between Spain and Portugal. *European Planning Studies* 26 (7): 1347–1365. https://doi.org/10.1080/09654313.2018.1464129.

Little, Peter D., Waktole Tiki, and Dejene Negassa Debsu. 2015. Formal or informal, legal or illegal: The ambiguous nature of cross-border Livestock Trade in the Horn of Africa. *Journal of Borderlands Studies* 30 (3): 405–421. https://doi.org/10.1080/08865655.2015.1068206.

Lundquist, Karl-Johan., and Michaela Trippl. 2013. Distance, proximity and types of cross-border innovation systems: A conceptual analysis. *Regional Studies* 47 (3): 450–460. https://doi.org/10.1080/00343404.2011.560933.

Lynch, Catherine. 2005. The PEACE II programme in Northern Ireland and the border counties: A 'distinctive' development programme? *Journal of Peacebuilding & Development* 2 (2): 59–76. https://doi.org/10.1080/15423166.2005.703778278935.

Malamud, Andres. 2013. *Overlapping regionalism, no integration: Conceptual issues and the Latin American Experiences*. 20. EUI RSCAS, Global Governance Programme-42. European University Institute (EUI). https://hdl.handle.net/1814/26336.

Manero, Edgardo A. 2007. Strategic representations, territory and border areas: Latin America and global disorder. *Geopolitics* 12 (1): 19–56. https://doi.org/10.1080/14650040601031123.

McCall, Cathal. 2011. Culture and the Irish border: Spaces for conflict transformation. *Cooperation and Conflict* 46 (2): 201–221. https://doi.org/10.1177/0010836711406406.

McCall, Cathal, and Xabier Itçaina. 2017. Secondary foreign policy activities in third sector cross-border cooperation as conflict transformation in the European Union: The cases of the Basque and Irish Borderscapes. *Regional & Federal Studies* 27 (3): 261–281. https://doi.org/10.1080/13597566.2017.1343723.

Medeiros, Eduardo. 2013. Euro–Meso–Macro: The new regions in Iberian and European space. *Regional Studies* 47 (8): 1249–1266. https://doi.org/10.1080/00343404.2011.602336.

Meijerink, Sander. 2014. Crossing borders, creating and managing cross-border regional alliances: Practical handbook to the crossing borders theory. *Journal of Borderlands Studies* 29 (4): 525–525. https://doi.org/10.1080/08865655.2014.982987.

Melious, Jean. 2006. *Governance of Canadian and American Ports*. 51. Border Policy Research Institute Publications. https://cedar.wwu.edu/bpri_publications/51.

MERCOSUR. 2021. DEC 020/2021 Presupuesto FOCEM 2022–2027. Montevideo, Uruguay: Fondo para la Convergencia Estructural del MERCOSUR (FOCEM). https://focem.mercosur.int/uploads/normativa/DEC_020-2021_ES_Presupuesto%20FOCEM%202022-7.pdf.

Mikhailova, Ekaterina. 2018. Collaborative problem-solving in the cross-border context: Learning from paired local communities along the Russian border. *Journal of Borderlands Studies* 33 (3): 445–464. https://doi.org/10.1080/08865655.2016.1195702.

Mirwaldt, Katja. 2012. The small projects fund and social capital formation in the Polish-German border region: An initial appraisal. *Regional Studies* 46 (2): 259–272. https://doi.org/10.1080/00343404.2010.490210.

Moscato, Derek. 2023. *Appeals to transboundary ecology: Cross-border advocacy at the Skagit Headwaters Donut Hole.* 134. Border Policy Research Institute Publications. https://cedar.wwu.edu/bpri_publications/134.

Mumme, Stephen P., and Pamela Duncan. 1996. The commission on environmental cooperation and the U.S.-Mexico border environment. *The Journal of Environment & Development* 5 (2): 197–215. https://doi.org/10.1177/107049659600500205.

Nadalutti, Elisabetta, and Jürgen Rüland. 2024. Cross-border regionalism in the EU and ASEAN: Another dimension of the 'Varieties of Regionalism.' *Journal of European Integration* March: 1–22. https://doi.org/10.1080/07036337.2024.2329636.

Niyazbekova, Shakizada, Oksana Nazarenko, Konstantin Bunevich, and Olga Ivanova. 2019. Special economic zones in Russia: Analysis, problems, and solutions [in Russian]. *Nauchnyi Vestnik: Finansy, Banki, Investitsii.*

Noferini, Andrea, Matteo Berzi, Francesco Camonita, and Antoni Durà. 2020. Cross-border cooperation in the EU: Euroregions amid multilevel governance and re-territorialization. *European Planning Studies* 28 (1): 35–56. https://doi.org/10.1080/09654313.2019.1623973.

Nshimbi, Christopher Changwe. 2015. Networks of cross-border non-state actors: The role of social capital in regional integration. *Journal of Borderlands Studies* 30 (4): 537–560. https://doi.org/10.1080/08865655.2016.1165131.

Nugent, Paul, and Isabella Soi. 2020. One-stop border posts in East Africa: State encounters of the Fourth Kind. *Journal of Eastern African Studies* 14 (3): 433–454. https://doi.org/10.1080/17531055.2020.1768468.

O'Neill, Maria. 2015. Security cooperation, counterterrorism, and EU–North Africa cross-border security relations, a legal perspective. *European Security* 24 (3): 438–453. https://doi.org/10.1080/09662839.2015.1028189.

O'Shea, Michael. 2023. *Jay Treaty and indigenous student mobility across the Canada-U.S. border: A focus on the cascadia region.* 138. Border Policy Research Institute Publications. https://cedar.wwu.edu/bpri_publications/138.

Oddone, Nahuel, and Horacio Rodríguez Vázquez. 2015. Cross-border paradiplomacy in Latin America. *Latin American Policy* 6 (1): 110–123. https://doi.org/10.1111/lamp.12059.

Ogalo, Victor. 2010. *Informal cross-border trade in EAC: Implications for regional integration and development.* Geneva, Switzerland: CUTS Geneva Resource Centre. https://www.wcoesarocb.org/wp-content/uploads/2018/07/Informal-Cross-Border-Trade-in-EAC-Implications-for-Regional-Intergration-Development.pdf.

Okechukwu, Richard Oji. 2018. Nigeria Niger Joint Commission for Cooperation (NNJCC): A model for the cross border cooperation initiative of the African Union border programme. *South East Political Review.*

Opioła, Wojciech, and Hynek Böhm. 2022. Euroregions as political actors: Managing border policies in the time of Covid-19 in Polish borderlands. *Territory, Politics, Governance* 10 (6): 896–916. https://doi.org/10.1080/21622671.2021.2017339.

Pacific NorthWest Economic Region. n.d. PNWER. https://www.pnwer.org/. Accessed 24 Nov 2024.

Peel, Deborah, and Michael Gregory Lloyd. 2015. Towards a framework for cooperation: Spatial public policy diplomacy on the Island of Ireland. *European Planning Studies* 23 (11): 2210–2226. https://doi.org/10.1080/09654313.2014.942601.

Perkmann, Markus. 2007a. Construction of new territorial scales: A framework and case study of the EUREGIO cross-border region. *Regional Studies* 41 (2): 253–266. https://doi.org/10.1080/00343400600990517.

Perkmann, Markus. 2007b. Policy entrepreneurship and multilevel governance: A comparative study of European cross-border regions. *Environment and Planning C: Government and Policy* 25 (6): 861–879. https://doi.org/10.1068/c60m.

References

Perrier Bruslé, Laetitia. 2013. The border as a marker of territoriality: Multi-scalar perspectives and multi-agent processes in a South American Borderland region. *Geopolitics* 18 (3): 584–611. https://doi.org/10.1080/14650045.2012.749242.

Pestsov, Sergey K., and Andrei B. Volynchuk. 2020. Cross-border cooperation in the strategy to 'revitalize' Northeast China [in Russian]. *Journal of Frontier Studies* 5 (4): 330–343. https://doi.org/10.46539/jfs.v5i4.223.

Peyrouse, Sebastien, and Gaël. Raballand. 2015. Central Asia: The new silk road initiative's questionable economic rationality. *Eurasian Geography and Economics* 56 (4): 405–420. https://doi.org/10.1080/15387216.2015.1114424.

Pipkin, Seth. 2018. Cashable value: Social capital and practical habits in the analysis of collaborative cross-border economic development. *Journal of Borderlands Studies* 33 (3): 329–350. https://doi.org/10.1080/08865655.2016.1197789.

Pires, Iva, and Flávio. Nunes. 2018. Labour mobility in the Euroregion Galicia-Norte de Portugal: Constraints faced by cross-border commuters. *European Planning Studies* 26 (2): 376–395. https://doi.org/10.1080/09654313.2017.1404968.

Plümmer, Franziska. 2022. Contested administrative capacity in border management: China and the Greater Mekong Subregion. *China Information* 36 (3): 407–429. https://doi.org/10.1177/0920203X221103053.

Prokkola, Eeva-Kaisa., and Maria Lois. 2016. Scalar politics of border heritage: An examination of the EU's Northern and Southern border areas. *Scandinavian Journal of Hospitality and Tourism* 16 (sup1): 14–35. https://doi.org/10.1080/15022250.2016.1244505.

Public Safety Canada. 2018. Beyond the border. December 21. https://www.publicsafety.gc.ca/cnt/brdr-strtgs/bynd-th-brdr/index-en.aspx.

Regulation - 883/2004 - EN - EUR-Lex. n.d. https://eur-lex.europa.eu/legal-content/EN/TXT/?uri=celex%3A32004R0883. Accessed 14 Nov 2024.

Renner, T., S. Meijerink, and P. Van Der Zaag. 2018. The evolution of regional cross-border water regimes, the Case of Deltarhine. *Journal of Environmental Planning and Management* 61 (10): 1701–1721. https://doi.org/10.1080/09640568.2017.1371005.

República Argentina y República Federativa de Brasil. 2009. *Acuerdo Entre La República Argentina y La República Federativa de Brasil Sobre Localidades Fronterizas Vinculadas*. http://www.saij.gob.ar/26523-nacional-acuerdo-entre-republica-argentina-republica-federativa-brasil-sobre-localidades-fronterizas-vinculadas-lnt0005542-2009-10-14/123456789-0abc-defg-g24-55000tcanyel.

Revised Protocol to the Withdrawal Agreement. 2019. https://assets.publishing.service.gov.uk/government/uploads/system/uploads/attachment_data/file/840230/Revised_Protocol_to_the_Withdrawal_Agreement.pdf.

Rhi-Sausi, José Luis., and Nahuel Oddone. 2012. Cross-border cooperation and regional integration: Opportunities to Peru. *The Perspective of the World Review* 4 (1): 147–172.

Rosanò, Alessandro. 2021. Perspectives of strengthened cooperation between cross-border regions: The European Commission's proposal of a regulation on the mechanism to resolve legal and administrative obstacles in the cross-border context. *Maastricht Journal of European and Comparative Law* 28 (4): 437–451. https://doi.org/10.1177/1023263X211010361.

Rumelili, Bahar. 2005. Civil society and the Europeanization of Greek-Turkish cooperation. *South European Society and Politics* 10 (1): 45–56. https://doi.org/10.1080/13608740500037940.

Rumford, Chris. 2014. *Cosmopolitan borders*. London: Palgrave Pivot.

Russian Federation. 2017. *Federal Law No. 179-FZ of July 26, 2017, on the Fundamentals of Cross-Border Cooperation (in Russian)*. https://economy.gov.ru/material/file/1654b44cb3682db35a43afe86/02e779/0001201707260027.pdf.

Rustamova, Leili. 2019. Problems and prospects of cross-border cooperation in Euroregions with Russia's participation [in Russian]. *Regionologiya* 4: 711–733.

San Diego Association of Governments. n.d. Borders Committee. San Diego Association of Governments. https://www.sandag.org/meetings-and-events/policy-advisory-committees/borders. Accessed 29 Nov 2024.

Säre, Margit. 2020. *Non-governmental organizations and cross-border environmental cooperation: Salish Sea and Baltic Sea Regions*. 118. Border Policy Research Institute Publications. Border Policy Research Institute. https://cedar.wwu.edu/bpri_publications/118.

Sarmiento-Mirwaldt, Katja, and Urszula Roman-Kamphaus. 2013. Cross-border cooperation in Central Europe: A comparison of culture and policy effectiveness in the Polish-German and Polish-Slovak Border Regions. *Europe-Asia Studies* 65 (8): 1621–1641. https://doi.org/10.1080/09668136.2013.832997.

Satyawan, Ignatius Agung. 2018. The benefit of joint border cooperation between Malaysia and Indonesia through Sosek-Malindo cooperation in North Kalimantan Province. The 6th Asian Academic Society International Conference (AASIC) A Transformative Community: Asia in Dynamism, Innovation, and Globalization.

Scheumann, Waltina, and Elke Herrfahrdt-Pähle, eds. 2008. *Conceptualizing cooperation on Africa's transboundary groundwater resources*. Bonn, Germany: Deutsches Institut für Entwicklungspolitik (DIE).

Scott, James Wesley. 1999. European and North American contexts for cross-border regionalism. *Regional Studies* 33 (7): 605–617. https://doi.org/10.1080/00343409950078657.

Scott, James Wesley. 2000. Transboundary cooperation on Germany's borders: Strategic regionalism through multilevel governance. *Journal of Borderlands Studies* 15 (1): 143–167. https://doi.org/10.1080/08865655.2000.9695545.

Scott, James Wesley. 2017. Cross-border, transnational, and interregional cooperation. In *The International Encyclopaedia of Geography: People, the earth, environment, and technology*, edited by Douglas Richardson, Noel Castree, Michael Goodchild, Audrey Kobayashi, Weidong Liu, and Richard Marston. Malden, MA: John Wiley & Sons, Ltd.

SEUPB. n.d. PEACE PLUS Programme. https://peaceplatform.seupb.eu/en/. Accessed 14 Nov 2024.

Shen, Jianfa. 2004. Cross-border urban governance in Hong Kong: The role of state in a globalizing city-region. *The Professional Geographer* 56 (4): 530–543. https://doi.org/10.1111/j.0033-0124.2004.00446.x.

Shepherd, Jack, and Dimitri Ioannides. 2020. Useful funds, disappointing framework: Tourism stakeholder experiences of INTERREG. *Scandinavian Journal of Hospitality and Tourism* 20 (5): 485–502. https://doi.org/10.1080/15022250.2020.1792339.

Smart, Alan, and George Lin. 2004. Border management and growth coalitions in the Hong Kong transborder region. *Identities* 11 (3): 377–396. https://doi.org/10.1080/10702890490493545.

Sohn, Christophe. 2014. Modelling cross-border integration: The role of borders as a resource. *Geopolitics* 19 (3): 587–608. https://doi.org/10.1080/14650045.2014.913029.

Sohn, Christophe. 2023. The impact of rebordering on cross-border cooperation actors' discourses in the Öresund Region. A semantic network approach. *Geografiska Annaler: Series B, Human Geography*, October, 1–23. https://doi.org/10.1080/04353684.2023.2266436.

Spierings, Bas, and Martin Van Der Velde. 2013. Cross-border mobility, unfamiliarity and development policy in Europe. *European Planning Studies* 21 (1): 1–4. https://doi.org/10.1080/09654313.2012.716235.

Startsev, A. 2016. The 'Great Altai' project: Historical retrospective and modern condition [in Russian]. *Razvitie Territoriy*.

Stefanick, Lorna. 2009. Transboundary conservation: Security, civil society and cross-border collaboration. *Journal of Borderlands Studies* 24 (2): 15–37. https://doi.org/10.1080/08865655.2009.9695725.

Su, Xiaobo. 2013. From frontier to bridgehead: Cross-border regions and the experience of Y Unnan, C Hina. *International Journal of Urban and Regional Research* 37 (4): 1213–1232. https://doi.org/10.1111/j.1468-2427.2012.01191.x.

Svensson, Sara, and Carl Nordlund. 2015. The building blocks of a Euroregion: Novel metrics to measure cross-border integration. *Journal of European Integration* 37 (3): 371–389. https://doi.org/10.1080/07036337.2014.968568.

References

Tangseefa, Decha. 2018. Border economies in the Greater Mekong sub-region. *Journal of Borderlands Studies* 33 (3): 509–510. https://doi.org/10.1080/08865655.2016.1204935.

Tannam, Etain. 2006. Cross-border co-operation between Northern Ireland and the Republic of Ireland: Neo-functionalism revisited. *The British Journal of Politics and International Relations* 8 (2): 256–276. https://doi.org/10.1111/j.1467-856X.2006.00202.x.

Tannam, Etain. 2007. The European Commission's evolving role in conflict resolution: The case of Northern Ireland 1989–2005. *Cooperation and Conflict* 42 (3): 337–356. https://doi.org/10.1177/0010836707079936.

Terlouw, Kees. 2012. Border surfers and Euroregions: Unplanned cross-border behaviour and planned territorial structures of cross-border governance. *Planning Practice and Research* 27 (3): 351–366. https://doi.org/10.1080/02697459.2012.670939.

The University of British Columbia. n.d. Advancing the cascadia innovation corridor | Innovation UBC. The University of British Columbia. https://innovation.ubc.ca/innovation-stories/advancing-cascadia-innovation-corridor. Accessed 25 Nov 2024.

The White House. 2002. U.S.- Canada smart border/30 point action plan update. The White House Archives. December 6. https://georgewbush-whitehouse.archives.gov/news/releases/2002/12/20021206-1.html.

Tijuana EDC. 2020. What Is the Cali Baja Mega Region? Cooperation for Business, June 4, Tijuana EDC edition. https://tijuanaedc.org/what-is-the-cali-baja-mega-region-cooperation-for-business/.

Timothy, Dallen J. 1999. Cross-border partnership in tourism resource management: International parks along the US-Canada border. *Journal of Sustainable Tourism* 7 (3–4): 182–205. https://doi.org/10.1080/09669589908667336.

Tochkov, Kiril. 2022. Trade efficiency, cross-border integration, and regional barriers in Northeast China. *The Chinese Economy* 55 (1): 13–25. https://doi.org/10.1080/10971475.2021.1892921.

Tomassian, Georgina Cipoletta. 2015. Financiamiento de La Infraestructura Para La Integración Regional: Alternativas Para América Del Sur. 259. Santiago de Chile: Comisión Económica para América Latina y el Caribe (CEPAL). https://repositorio.cepal.org/server/api/core/bitstreams/a237b589-d4bd-4d3e-a6f9-12aa9e9c3c1b/content.

Trautman, Laurie, Francesco Cappellano, and Border Policy Research Institute. 2019. The cascadia innovation corridor: Advancing a cross-border economy. *Border Policy Research Institute Publications*, no. 117. https://cedar.wwu.edu/bpri_publications/117.

Treaty relating to cooperative development of the water resources of the Columbia River Basin (with Annexes). 1961. https://web.archive.org/web/20100706215743/http://www.ccrh.org/comm/river/docs/cotreaty.htm.

Tsuji, Hisako. 2004. *The Tumen River area development programme: Its history and current status as of 2004*. Niigata, Japan: Economic Research Institute for Northeast Asia (ERINA). https://www.unii.ac.jp/erina-unp/archive/en/wp-content/uploads/2018/05/DP0404e.pdf.

U.S. Customs and Border Protection. n.d.-b. "NEXUS." https://www.cbp.gov/travel/trusted-traveler-programs/nexus. Accessed 20 Nov 2024.

U.S. Customs and Border Protection. n.d.-a. FAST: free and secure trade for commercial vehicles | U.S. customs and border protection. https://www.cbp.gov/travel/trusted-traveler-programs/fast. Accessed 20 Nov 2024.

Van Winsen, Bart. 2009. Political cooperation in EUREGIO: Democratic dimensions in cross-border cooperation. *European View* 8 (1): 153–161. https://doi.org/10.1007/s12290-009-0079-5.

Villanueva, Wong, L. Jose, Tetsuo Kidokoro, and Fumihiko Seta. 2023. A governance theory for cross-border regions: Identifying principles and processes with grounded theory. *Journal of Borderlands Studies* 38 (1): 95–118. https://doi.org/10.1080/08865655.2021.1878924.

Wassenberg, Birte. 2017. Secondary Foreign Policy as a peace-building tool: A European model? The contribution of cross-border cooperation to reconciliation and stability in Europe. *Regional & Federal Studies* 27 (3): 219–237. https://doi.org/10.1080/13597566.2017.1343720.

Więckowski, Marek. 2023. How border tripoints offer opportunities for transboundary tourism development. *Tourism Geographies* 25 (1): 310–333. https://doi.org/10.1080/14616688.2021.1878268.

Wilson, Thomas. 2000. The obstacles to European Union regional policy in the Northern Ireland borderlands. *Human Organization* 59 (1): 1–10. https://doi.org/10.17730/humo.59.1.d4725058w3g38773.

Y2Y. 2024. "Landscape Protection." Yellowstone to Yukon Conservation Initiative. June 14. https://y2y.net/landscape-protection/.

Yakhlef, Sophia, Goran Basic, and Malin Akerstrom. 2017. Policing migration: Described and observed cooperation experiences of police and border guards in the Baltic Sea Area. *Journal of Applied Security Research* 12 (1): 117–140. https://doi.org/10.1080/19361610.2017.1228422.

Yang, Chun. 2006. The geopolitics of cross-boundary governance in the Greater Pearl River Delta, China: A case study of the proposed Hong Kong–Zhuhai–Macao Bridge. *Political Geography* 25 (7): 817–835. https://doi.org/10.1016/j.polgeo.2006.08.006.

Yang, Chun, and Si-ming Li. 2013. Transformation of cross-boundary governance in the Greater Pearl River Delta, China: Contested geopolitics and emerging conflicts. *Habitat International* 40 (October): 25–34. https://doi.org/10.1016/j.habitatint.2013.02.001.

Yndigegn, Carsten. 2013. Reviving unfamiliarity—The Case of public resistance to the establishment of the Danish-German Euroregion. *European Planning Studies* 21 (1): 58–74. https://doi.org/10.1080/09654313.2012.716239.

Zanker, Franzisca, Kwaku Arhin-Sam, Amanda Bisong, and Leonie Jegen. 2020. *Free movement in West Africa: Juxtapositions and divergent interests*. 1. Policy Brief. Kiel, Germany: Mercator Dialogue on Migration and Asylum (MEDAM). https://ecdpm.org/application/files/6316/5546/8622/MEDAM_PolicyBrief_ECOWAS.pdf.

Zhurzhenko, Tatiana. 2004. Cross-border cooperation and transformation of regional identities in the Ukrainian-Russian borderlands: Towards a Euroregion 'Slobozhanshchyna'? Part 1. *Nationalities Papers* 32 (1): 207–232. https://doi.org/10.1080/0090599042000186133.

Open Access This chapter is licensed under the terms of the Creative Commons Attribution 4.0 International License (http://creativecommons.org/licenses/by/4.0/), which permits use, sharing, adaptation, distribution and reproduction in any medium or format, as long as you give appropriate credit to the original author(s) and the source, provide a link to the Creative Commons license and indicate if changes were made.

The images or other third party material in this chapter are included in the chapter's Creative Commons license, unless indicated otherwise in a credit line to the material. If material is not included in the chapter's Creative Commons license and your intended use is not permitted by statutory regulation or exceeds the permitted use, you will need to obtain permission directly from the copyright holder.

Chapter 3
Central Asian Cross-Border Cooperation

3.1 Overview

Central Asia, as a region, took its current shape in the aftermath of the Soviet Union's collapse in 1991. The decision to formally designate the region as "Central Asia" was made in January 1993 during a meeting in Tashkent, where representatives of Kazakhstan, Kyrgyzstan, Tajikistan, Turkmenistan, and Uzbekistan agreed to replace the Soviet-era term "Middle Asia and Kazakhstan" ("*Sredniaia Aziia i Kazakhstan*") (Rosset and Svarin 2014).

The newly emerged five states inherited extensive legacies from their shared Soviet past. At the outset of their independence, they shared numerous commonalities, including operational aspects such as centralized governance practices, interdependent economies, intertwined transportation networks, and an integrated power grid system (e.g., Collins 2009; Aminjonov 2016). In addition, the region shares ideational elements and cultural affinities, including overlapping identities rooted in linguistic and religious traditions shaped by ethnic and kinship ties. Linguistic affinities are particularly pronounced among the Turkic-speaking nations, with Persian-speaking Tajikistan as the exception. Russian, meanwhile, continues to serve as a common lingua franca across the region, being used for official negotiations and other cross-border interactions, which, among other things, facilitates cross-border cooperation. Religious traditions further unite the region, as the majority of the population practices Sunni Islam of the Hanafi school of Islamic jurisprudence (mazhab).

In the international political context, *regional integration* has occupied a prominent place in the region's political agenda since the 1990s. However, efforts at regional self-organization, such as the now-defunct Central Asian Cooperation Organization, so far have largely been unsuccessful. Instead, the Central Asian states have gravitated toward multilateral frameworks dominated by extra-regional powers like Russia and China, such as the Eurasian Economic Union (EAEU), the Collective Security Treaty Organization (CSTO), and the Shanghai Cooperation Organization (SCO).

© The Author(s) 2025
S. Golunov and A. Bitabar, *Bridging Borders*,
SpringerBriefs in Political Science, https://doi.org/10.1007/978-3-031-84253-5_3

This dynamic has led many scholars to characterize Central Asian integration as limited, or even as "failed" or "virtual" (Moldashev and Qoraboyev 2018; Buranelli 2021). Recent scholarship has partially revisited this pessimistic stance, particularly in light of the 2016 leadership change in Uzbekistan. The policy of the new administration of President Mirziyoyev, which has prioritized strengthening ties with neighboring states, has served as a catalyst for renewed efforts to enhance the country's bilateral relations and foster broader multilateral cooperation within the region. The initiation of consultative meetings among the five Central Asian states marks a significant step in this process. Scholars now contend that Central Asian cooperation should not be evaluated solely through the framework of formal organizations. Instead, they highlight the increasing relevance of informal practices and mechanisms that facilitate collaboration among Central Asian states, even amid historical fluctuations in their relationships (Moldashev and Qoraboyev 2018; Buranelli 2021). Anyway, even being in its nascent stage—somewhat comparable to the pre-European Coal and Steel Community phase of the European integration—Central Asian integration nonetheless provides a favorable political backdrop for CBC. The importance of fostering cooperation between regional authorities and business communities, establishing trade and production zones at border areas, and promoting transit has been emphasized on multiple occasions during meetings of Central Asian leaders (Akorda 2021).

Extra-regional actors, including great powers and international organizations, also play a significant role in promoting intraregional cooperation. Notable examples include the Asian Development Bank led CAREC program and China's Belt and Road Initiative, which have contributed to infrastructure development and enhanced connectivity across the region. In the current temporal context, the Middle Corridor passing through Central Asia has gained growing strategic importance. Such initiatives, among other things, can incentivize the development of intraregional cross-border infrastructures, which is important for advancing regional CBC.

Governance in Central Asia remains highly centralized, with all five states exhibiting varying degrees of authoritarianism. Neopatrimonial and nationalizing tendencies reinforce this centralization, with regime security and sovereignty consistently prioritized over bilateral cooperation or regional integration. Leaders view sovereignty and control over strategic resources as paramount, fearing that initiatives like pooling sovereignty or easing border controls could undermine their authority. In other words, central authorities are typically reluctant to delegate special powers or allocate significant funding to border regions, creating additional barriers to effective cross-border cooperation. Fears of instability and internal violence further discourage cooperation with neighbors perceived as unreliable. For instance, Turkmenistan, the region's most closed and restrictive state, has adhered to a policy of permanent neutrality since 1995, significantly limiting its engagement with the region. Similarly, Uzbekistan often had strained relations with its neighbors during Islam Karimov's rule, particularly in the late 2000s, which created significant obstacles to cross-border cooperation. Furthermore, nation-building has frequently been prioritized over region-building, diminishing the prospects for meaningful regional integration (e.g., Collins 2009; Megoran 2017; Buranelli 2021). For similar reasons,

3.1 Overview

the leaderships of Central Asian countries likely view civic activism—particularly cross-border activism—with a degree of suspicion.

Still, cross-border (or bilateral interregional) cooperation is explicitly identified as a priority in some framework agreements between Central Asian countries, often expressed as a mutual commitment to encourage collaboration among provinces, districts, and other administrative units, as well as to foster people-to-people connections across borders. In several cases, official regional interactions among Central Asian states have shown trends toward intensification and institutionalization. By the end of 2024, six meetings of the Council of Heads of Border Regions had been held between Kyrgyzstan and Uzbekistan, four interregional forums were convened between Kazakhstan and Uzbekistan, two forums—between Turkmenistan and Uzbekistan and one forum—between Kazakhstan and Kyrgyzstan and between Tajikistan and Uzbekistan.

The development of cross-border interregional connections is, in some cases, facilitated by the *rotation of officials between leadership roles in embassies and border regions*. For instance, the appointment of Kazakhstan's ambassador to Uzbekistan as Akim (head) of Turkestan Region in 2022, the transfer of the Akim of Mangystau Region to the position of ambassador to Turkmenistan in 2024, and the assignment of a former Uzbek official who held various posts in Karakalpakstan as Uzbekistan's Consul General in Aktau in 2021 exemplify this practice. Such rotations provide appointees with an understanding of border region perspectives, equipping them with enhanced capacity to formally and informally advocate for the cross-border interests of these regions.

The development of *economic cooperation* among Central Asian countries is significantly affected by the fact that for none of these countries a neighboring state is their main trade partner. Central Asian economies are more influenced by external supply-and-demand factors than by internal regional trade and market interactions and the Central Asian foreign trade is heavily dominated by extra-regional powers, particularly Russia and China. This dependence is further reinforced by the use of Russian transportation routes, remittances from labor migrants in Russia, and significant investments from both Russia and China (Yusupov 2024). Meanwhile, intraregional trade remains limited, although it has shown growth since 2017, largely driven by Uzbekistan's liberalization of its foreign trade regime following Shavkat Mirziyoyev's rise to power (see Figs. 3.1 and 3.2). Moreover, Central Asian exports are poorly diversified, consisting largely of raw materials with only a small share of high value-added products (Yusupov 2024) (Fig. 3.3).

A substantial barrier to advancing CBC in Central Asia is *corruption*, which poses serious challenges to the successful implementation of joint initiatives. According to the 2023 Corruption Perception Index, Kazakhstan ranks 93rd, Uzbekistan 121st, Kyrgyzstan 141st, and Turkmenistan 170th out of 180 countries (Transparency International 2024). Still, as the previous part demonstrates, corruption, while challenging, is not an insurmountable barrier to successful CBC when addressed appropriately.

The landlocked position of Central Asian countries, particularly Uzbekistan's double-landlocked status (as it borders only other four Central Asian countries and

Fig. 3.1 Central Asia

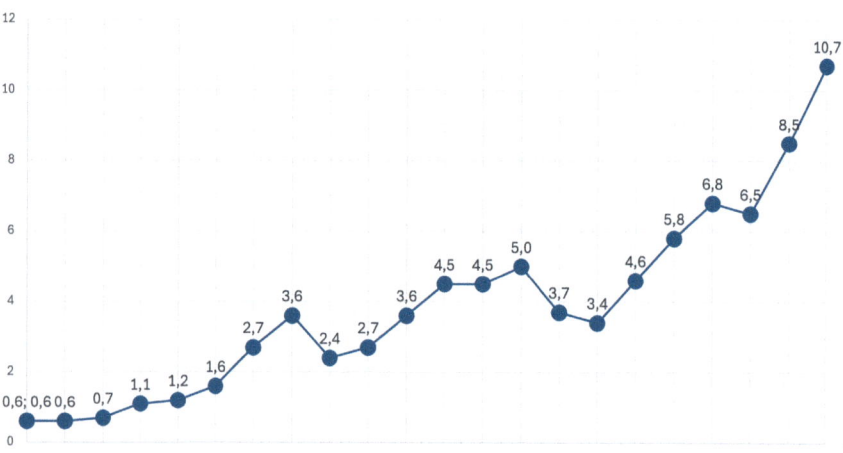

Fig. 3.2 Volumes of intranational goods exports within Central Asia (in billions USD) (*Source* Yusupov 2024, 14)

Afghanistan and has no direct access to any country with an ocean coastline), necessitates the development of international logistics corridors providing access to seaports This logistical challenge has worsened due to the Russian-Ukrainian war, which began in 2022, and the subsequent international sanctions on Russia. These developments have made transit from Central Asia through Russian territory to Western

3.1 Overview

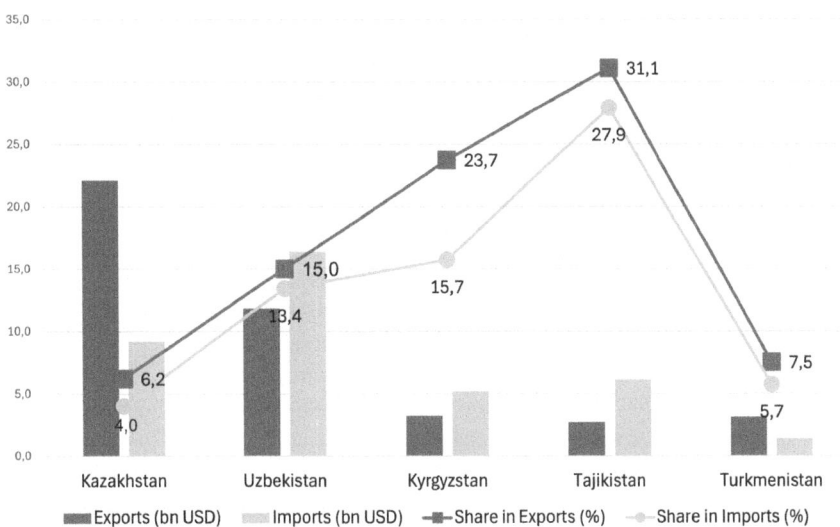

Fig. 3.3 Key indicators of intraregional trade of Central Asian countries for 2017–2022 (*Source* Yusupov 2024, 15)

markets significantly more complicated. Consequently, the search for alternative logistical corridors and the implementation of CBC infrastructure projects related to their development have become particularly important for Central Asian countries.

The conditions of landscape, transport, and demographic proximities vary significantly across different parts of Central Asia, leading to a sharp regional asymmetry in cross-border economic flows. The most relevant proximities for Central Asian CBC are not always defined by geographical closeness; instead, they are primarily driven by the mutual attraction of certain cities and the overall economic potential of neighboring regions.

While relatively large distances separate some cities linked by transport proximities, these are partially offset by the intensity of transport connections and the competitive market that lowers transportation costs. Examples of such proximities include Tashkent (Uzbekistan, 3 million) and Shymkent (Kazakhstan, 1.2 million); Almaty (Kazakhstan, 2 million) and Bishkek (Kyrgyzstan, 1.2 million); Tashkent and Khujand (Tajikistan, 200 thousand); Osh (Kyrgyzstan, 450 thousand) and Andijan (Uzbekistan, 400 thousand); Khujand and Bekabad (Uzbekistan, 100 thousand); and Samarkand (Uzbekistan, 570 thousand) and Penjikent (Tajikistan, 50 thousand). The potential of proximities involving Turkmenistan remains underutilized due to the country's strict regulation of entry and exit. This affects cities such as Khiva, Urgench, and Nukus (Uzbekistan, 650 thousand) and Dashoguz (Turkmenistan, 250 thousand), as well as Bukhara (Uzbekistan, 250 thousand) and Turkmenabad (Turkmenistan, 250 thousand).

In contrast, unfavorable landscape conditions, weak transport infrastructure, and, in some cases, the remoteness of major population centers from the border hinder

CBC in parts of the region's arid western zone (encompassing the borders of Kazakhstan, Uzbekistan, and Turkmenistan) as well as in the mountainous eastern zone, particularly affecting CBC between Kyrgyzstan and Tajikistan.

The cooperation between Central Asian countries is greatly affected by *distribution of natural resources* among them. In 2023, oil-rich Kazakhstan's GDP per capita was approximately $13,137 (World Bank 2023), while Tajikistan's GDP per capita stood at about $1189, reflecting its limited natural resource endowments and lower economic development levels (World Bank 2023). Similarly, Turkmenistan and Uzbekistan have abundant hydrocarbon resources.

In this context, it is important to highlight a key geographic and economic feature of the region: the divide between upstream and downstream countries regarding water resources. Kyrgyzstan and Tajikistan, situated upstream, control the headwaters of major rivers, while downstream nations—Kazakhstan, Turkmenistan, and Uzbekistan—depend on these water resources for agriculture and industry. This asymmetry generates both opportunities and challenges. Collaborative arrangements, such as water and water-energy exchange agreements, offer mechanisms to address shared needs. However, tensions frequently arise, particularly over seasonal water use for irrigation and hydropower. The allocation of scarce resources, including water, arable land, and pastures, poses a serious challenge for some Central Asian borderland areas, especially in Fergana Valley.

To address these complexities, effective CBC is essential. Balancing competing interests, ensuring mutually acceptable resource distribution, and strengthening collaboration are necessary steps to reduce conflicts and promote long-term stability both along borders and across the wider region. Resolving water-related challenges, closely intertwined with the management of mutual energy supplies, remains a key issue of interstate relations in Central Asia. At the local level, there is a need for the engagement of local communities and their institutions, such as water user associations, to address these issues constructively and peacefully.

Central Asia's *demographic landscape* is shaped by rapidly growing populations and predominantly young societies, which have a significant impact on cross-border cooperation. According to the Population Reference Bureau's (2023) World Population Data Sheet, the region's total fertility rate averages 3.2, reflecting steady population growth (Population Reference Bureau 2023). Additionally, 31% of the population is under the age of 15, demonstrating the youthfulness of these societies. This demographic structure creates both opportunities, such as a potential demographic dividend, and challenges, including pressures on education systems, job markets, and infrastructure.

In most Central Asian border regions where landscape and transport conditions favor CBC, population growth is evident, and, unlike the EU's borderlands, the issue of net population outflow is absent. Population growth is particularly evident in Fergana Valley, which spans Uzbekistan, Kyrgyzstan, and Tajikistan. This area is one of the most densely populated in Central Asia and has a large share of young people.

Population growth presents the challenge of providing employment for the expanding population, with likely avenues including cross-border trade (making

3.1 Overview

use of border markets) and agriculture. However, both options potentially introduce challenges, such as conflicts arising from intensified trade interactions, increased pressure on land and water resources, as well as corruption and criminal extortion in market activities.

As highlighted in several studies (Kaminski and Mitra 2012; Asian Development Bank 2020), one of the characteristic aspects of CBC in Central Asia is the *prevalence of informal cross-border trade* facilitated by local border markets, ranging from major hubs in Bishkek and Tashkent to smaller ones. At times, this trade has persisted even despite unfavorable conditions imposed by governments. The ineffective regulation of informal cross-border trade, coupled with periodic attempts to suppress it, has occasionally led to the proliferation of illicit practices, criminal activities surrounding border markets, and corruption, while also heightening the risk of cross-border conflicts. As noted earlier, creating favorable conditions for informal cross-border trade, alongside its proper regulation, could play a critical role in stabilizing border areas in the region, particularly in the context of demographic growth.

An important factor in Central Asian cross-border cooperation is the *contribution of international organizations and programs* such as UN agencies, European Union initiatives, the World Bank, the Asian Development Bank, and others. Their efforts are aimed at developing transport corridors, improving border management, protecting the environment, and supporting local communities, particularly in the Fergana Valley—the potentially most conflict-prone subregion of post-Soviet Central Asia, which occupies only 0.5% of the region's area but is home to 15% of its population. For instance, connectivity improvements in the region are being addressed by programs of the World Bank and the Asian Development Bank (World Bank n.d.), support for local communities is provided by UN agencies, and border management (including measures to reduce border delays and facilitate trade), as well as small projects supporting border communities in their areas of activity since the 2020s, is handled by the EU-funded BOMCA program (BOMCA n.d.). Environmental protection projects are supported by UN programs and the World Bank (UNDP n.d.-a; World Bank 2021).

Support from international organizations and programs helps define cooperation priorities and provides not only financial aid but also organizational assistance and expertise. However, it is not always successful. For instance, UN support and efforts by other organizations for local communities and conflict resolution in the Fergana Valley have been relatively successful in the Kyrgyz–Uzbek border areas, where in 2020, for example, the project "Joint Prosperity through Cooperation in the Border Regions of Kyrgyzstan and Uzbekistan" was launched. This initiative focuses primarily on creating opportunities for economic cooperation and expanding opportunities for youth and women (FAO 2023). However, in the Kyrgyz–Tajik border area, the activities of UN agencies, represented by the "Cross-Border Cooperation for Sustainable Peace and Development" project (conducted from 2015 to 2019 and primarily aimed at establishing dialogue between conflicting communities [UNDP n.d.-b]), practically stalled due to the escalation of the Kyrgyz–Tajik conflict in 2022.

Next, we will examine the specifics CBC in individual Central Asian states. Structuring such an overview presents certain challenges, as it is important to avoid overlapping analyses of the same border regions in different country-specific sections. Consequently, the length of the reviews on CBC issues in Central Asian countries will vary significantly: Toward the end of the chapter, these reviews will become shorter to prevent repetition.

3.2 Uzbekistan's Perspective

Today, Uzbekistan is the primary driving force behind not only post-2016 Central Asian cooperation efforts but also cross-border cooperation within the region. Tashkent's proactive diplomatic efforts toward its Central Asian neighbors in recent years have yielded significant progress, including the comprehensive resolution of border disputes, agreements on shared water resource management, the reopening and modernization of border checkpoints, and the relaxation of strict movement controls. Moreover, initiatives such as signing regional development programs for bordering areas, establishing border trade centers, and implementing policies to attract tourists have further strengthened these efforts. Together, these top-down measures have intensified and institutionalized cross-border cooperation along Uzbekistan's borders, solidifying its role as a linchpin in the region. This development will be analyzed in greater detail in this section.

Such progress can be seen as a natural consequence of Uzbekistan's geographic position. Uzbekistan lies at the heart of Central Asia and is uniquely the only country that shares borders with all other Central Asian states, making it central to regional connectivity and cooperation. Uzbekistan's borders with Central Asia cover substantial distances (though figures vary slightly across sources): approximately 2350 km with Kazakhstan (Tokaev and Amanzholova 2014, 151), slightly over 1300 km with Kyrgyzstan (Radio Azattyk 2023), approx. 1330 km with Tajikistan (Radio Ozodi 2024b), and 1650 km with Turkmenistan (Boyarov 2024). Besides its Central Asian neighbors, it also borders Afghanistan, a country mired in decades of violence and instability (Fig. 3.4).

Another key factor in Uzbekistan's role is its population size. With a population of about 37 million, Uzbekistan is Central Asia's largest market and a potential gravitational center for regional cooperation. The densely populated areas along its borders provide natural avenues for cross-border trade, labor mobility, and cultural exchange with neighboring countries (Statistics Agency under the President of the Republic of Uzbekistan 2024a). The country's ethnic and cultural composition further enhances this role. While Uzbekistan itself is home to diverse ethnic groups, the presence of significant Uzbek communities in neighboring states, collectively numbering around six million, establishes Uzbeks as the region's largest ethnic group. Moreover, Uzbekistan's military capacity, with the largest armed forces in Central Asia comprising approximately 50,000 active troops, further reinforces its strategic significance (Laumulin 2018).

3.2 Uzbekistan's Perspective

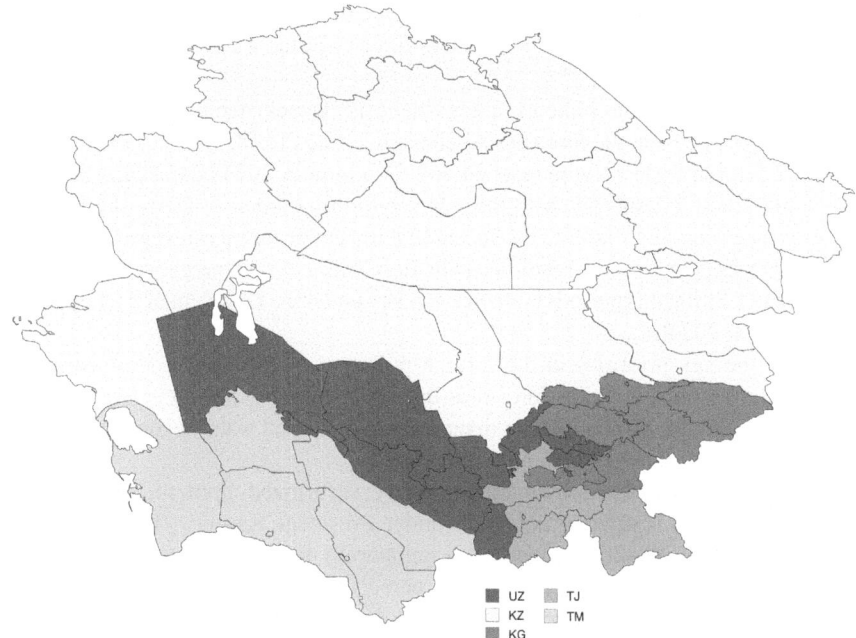

Fig. 3.4 Uzbekistan and neighboring Central Asian states

Given these geostrategic and geoeconomic, it would seem logical for Tashkent to prioritize building strong relations with its Central Asian neighbors. However, this was not the case during the *presidency of Islam Karimov*. Under his rule, Uzbekistan maintained a more closed (albeit stable and predictable) foreign policy and often had tense relations with neighboring states.

It was only after Karimov's death that Uzbekistan began to reassess the significance of its geographic centrality—and the vulnerabilities it entails—through concrete actions. Following *Shavkat Mirziyoyev's rise to power*, Uzbekistan has taken steps toward a more open and cooperative stance in regional and international affairs (Dadabaev 2019; Toktogulov 2022). Efforts have been made to liberalize the country's foreign trade regime and initiate substantial market-oriented reforms. These reforms include the unification of the exchange rate, liberalization of the foreign exchange market, introduction of price and trade liberalization measures in September 2017, and reductions in business and individual tax rates beginning in January 2019 (World Bank 2019).

Shortly after assuming office, President Mirziyoyev prioritized Central Asia in his foreign policy agenda. He articulated this commitment in his 2016 parliamentary address and reiterated at the United Nations General Assembly the following year (Mirziyoyev 2017). While structural reforms and the transformation of entrenched practices have presented challenges, Uzbekistan's relationships with its Central Asian neighbors have improved markedly since Mirziyoyev took office. Practical steps in this direction revitalized cross-border relations, as Uzbekistan's centralized governance ensures that top-level initiatives directly influence developments on the ground.

The effects of these policies are evident in Uzbekistan's *trade dynamics*. According to data from the Statistics Agency under the President of Uzbekistan, the country's foreign trade volume reached $62.57 billion in 2023 (Eurasianet 2022b). This figure contrasts sharply with the $24.2 billion recorded in 2016, the year of Karimov's passing, highlighting the substantial impact of recent reforms (Eurasianet 2022b). Uzbekistan's trade relations with its Central Asian neighbors have also strengthened during this period (Statistics Agency under the President of the Republic of Uzbekistan 2024b).

One of the key priorities in the foreign policy of Mirziyoyev's administration toward neighboring Central Asian states has been *resolving border-related issues*, ranging from border disputes to the management of shared water resources and the regulation of cross-border movement of people.

Historically, Uzbekistan maintained highly securitized borders, reflecting a cautious and often restrictive approach under President Karimov. Following the Batken events of 1999–2000, Uzbekistan unilaterally mined sections of its borders with Kyrgyzstan and Tajikistan to address perceived security threats from militant groups. While mines were removed from the Kyrgyz border in 2005 (ReliefWeb 2005), those along the Tajik border remained. Moreover, Uzbekistan introduced a visa regime for Tajik citizens in 2001. Further restrictions followed the Andijan events in 2005 and the Osh events in 2010, leading to the closure of several border checkpoints with Kyrgyzstan, which severely limited cross-border movement. Borders with both Kyrgyzstan and Tajikistan remained undelimited.

Uzbekistan holds a special place for Tajikistan due to their deep-rooted cultural, social, and economic proximities. For centuries, Turkic and Iranian speakers in this region have coexisted, intermarried, and shared traditions (Finke and Sancak 2012). Tajiks and Uzbeks are significant ethnic groups in both countries. While Uzbekistan hosts a substantial Tajik population, Uzbeks are a sizable ethnic group in Tajikistan. According to Tajikistan's 2010 national census, ethnic Uzbeks comprised 12.2% of the population, concentrated in the regions along the border with Uzbekistan (Minority Rights Group 2018). Tajikistan's statehood has been closely linked to its relationship with Uzbekistan, often perceived as its most significant "Other" (Suyarkulova 2012). The densely populated border between the two countries features the highest number of border crossings for Tajikistan, totaling 16 (Ministry of Foreign Affairs of the Republic of Tajikistan 2013). Moreover, Uzbekistan was once Tajikistan's main trading partner, with bilateral trade turnover reaching $250 million in 1995—twice the combined trade with all other CIS countries (Chorshanbiev 2023).

However, as relations began to worsen in the late 1990s, trade volumes drastically declined, with transport connections being severed and some sections of the border mined. During periods of heightened tension, Tajikistan experienced economic blockades, exacerbating its isolation and hindering economic development.

3.2 Uzbekistan's Perspective

Relations with Tajikistan became particularly tense after Tajikistan's 2008 announcement of plans to construct the Rogun hydropower plant, which raised concerns in downstream Uzbekistan regarding water resources.

In a similar vein, restrictions were imposed on Uzbekistan's borders with Kazakhstan and Turkmenistan. Although a visa-free regime was in place between Uzbekistan and Kazakhstan, and a limited visa-free arrangement introduced in 2004 permitted Uzbek and Turkmen residents in border areas to travel for up to three days without a visa, mobility was often hampered by periodic border closures. For instance, from 2013 to 2017, the border with Turkmenistan was closed, and the visa-free regime was suspended (Radio Ozodlik 2017). Moreover, when Mirziyoyev took office, Uzbekistan had undelimited borders with Kyrgyzstan and Tajikistan. Addressing these issues became a key priority.

During Islam Karimov's presidency, border delimitation was completed only with Kazakhstan and Turkmenistan. Under Mirziyoyev, the demarcation process with Kazakhstan was finalized, while efforts with Turkmenistan were resumed and remain ongoing.

Tashkent's commitment and determination are evident in the completion of border delimitation with both Kyrgyzstan and Tajikistan. In January 2023, Uzbek and Kyrgyz leaders exchanged ratification instruments for an additional border agreement signed in November 2022, which resolved lingering disputes, including issues related to enclaves or exclaves and water resources (Rickleton 2023). A key part of this agreement was the transfer of the Kempir-Abad reservoir—referred to as Andijan in Uzbekistan—located near the border at the intersection of Kyrgyzstan's Jalal-Abad and Osh regions and Uzbekistan's Andijan region, to Uzbekistan. A separate agreement was reached on joint water management, reportedly ensuring that the Kyrgyz side could continue to use the reservoir (Radio Azattyk 2022). Experts estimate that 14% of Kempir–Abad reservoir water irrigates Kyrgyzstan's Suzak and Kara-Suu districts, while for Uzbekistan, it supports over two million hectares of farmland (CABAR.asia 2023).

Another outcome of this deal was the integration of Barak, a Kyrgyz exclave entirely surrounded by Uzbekistan, into Uzbek territory. In exchange, Kyrgyzstan received an equivalent parcel of land from Uzbekistan's Andijan Province. This resolution addressed long-standing challenges faced by Barak's residents, who had struggled with restricted access to Kyrgyzstan due to strict border controls that hindered travel and trade (Rickleton 2024). Assessing this development, Shavkat Mirziyoyev emphasized that "the comprehensive resolution of the border delimitation issue" would play an important role in advancing cross-border collaboration and strengthening regional cooperation (President.uz 2023).

Border delimitation with Tajikistan had been completed earlier, reportedly in 2019 (Radio Ozodi 2024b). Similar to the Uzbek–Kyrgyz border settlement, the management of shared water resources and facilities was a central issue in negotiations with Tajikistan. The Farhod hydrocomplex, encompassing the hydroelectric power plant and reservoir, de-facto controlled by Tajikistan, was a long-standing source of tension between Dushanbe and Tashkent, as both nations claimed the disputed border area along the Syrdarya River. In August 2018, Tajikistan and Uzbekistan formalized an agreement resolving the dispute over the Farhod hydrocomplex. The dam and its territory were recognized as part of Tajikistan, while the hydroelectric power station was transferred to Uzbekistan. Tajikistan assumed responsibility for security, and Uzbekistan took charge of maintenance, establishing a collaborative framework that ended years of contention (CABAR.asia 2021). Furthermore, in early 2020, Uzbekistan announced it had finished removing mines along its border with Tajikistan. This marked a significant step, as the mined border had caused severe harm: According to Tajik sources, more than 800 residents were injured or killed by mine explosions over the past two decades (Radio Free Europe/Radio Liberty 2020).

Water management has long played a central role in shaping Uzbekistan's relations with its neighbors. Since the early 1990s, there have been concerted efforts to establish institutions and mechanisms for transboundary water management in Central Asia, particularly concerning the waters of the Amu Darya and Syr Darya rivers (Mukhammadiev 2014).

One notable recent development in this context is Uzbekistan's shift in stance toward Tajikistan's Rogun Dam project, which had been a major source of tension and a contributing factor to strained bilateral relations since the late 2000s. Under President Mirziyoyev's administration, Uzbekistan adopted a more conciliatory approach by refraining from criticizing the Rogun project. Remarkably, in June 2022, Uzbekistan reportedly committed to purchasing electricity generated by the dam during the summer months, when hydroelectric production is at its peak (Eurasianet 2022a).

Uzbekistan has also strengthened transboundary water cooperation through agreements on the 2017 Orto-Tokoy (also known as "Kasansay" in Uzbekistan) Reservoir with Kyrgyzstan (Kudryavtseva 2017), joint modernization efforts for the Tuyamuyun Hydroelectric Complex with Turkmenistan in 2021–2022 (Carececo.org 2022), and the installation of water meters on the Syr Darya with Kazakhstan in 2024 (Putz 2024). Furthermore, collaboration with Kazakhstan in addressing the aftermath of the Sardoba dam failure in 2020 highlights the importance of coordinated disaster response (Genevawaterhub.org 2020).

Regarding *cross-border movement and trade*, the recent reopening and modernization of border checkpoints, along with the relaxation of border crossing regimes, have played a crucial role in fostering closer ties between Uzbekistan and its Central Asian neighbors, signaling a shift toward greater openness and mobility.

This shift toward greater openness and mobility is exemplified by several key developments. In 2017, the border with Turkmenistan reopened, and a visa-free regime for border residents was reinstated, reflecting efforts to enhance regional connectivity. In September 2023, two border checkpoints between Kyrgyzstan and Uzbekistan—"Begabad-avtodorozhnyi" and "Kara-Bagysh-avtodorozhnyi"—were reopened, marking a significant step toward improving cross-border connectivity (Radio Ozodi 2024a). A year later, in September 2024, the reopening of two additional checkpoints—"Karasuu" in the Osh region and "Ken-say" in the Jalalabad region—restored crossings that had been closed since 2010, representing a new milestone in bilateral relations (Nurmatov 2024). With these developments, the total number of operational border checkpoints on the Kyrgyz side reached 13. Kyrgyz authorities have further announced plans to open additional checkpoints in the Osh

3.2 Uzbekistan's Perspective

region, including the Yntymak checkpoint, which is currently under reconstruction. On the Uzbekistan–Kazakhstan border, checkpoints are undergoing reconstruction to triple their capacity (Spot.uz 2024a).

Reconnection with Tajikistan has seen particularly remarkable improvement. In 2018, Presidents Emomali Rahmon and Shavkat Mirziyoyev exchanged visits, with Mirziyoyev's visit to Tajikistan being the first by an Uzbek leader in two decades. The signing of the 2018 Treaty on Strategic Partnership not only formalized this rapprochement but also led to tangible measures such as the completion of border delimitation, reopening of border crossings, removal of mines, and restoration and further enhancement of transportation links between the two countries.

The signing of cooperation agreements and roadmaps for 2024–2026 between the executive authorities of Khatlon and Sughd Provinces of Tajikistan and those of Khorezm, Fergana, Syrdarya, Namangan, and Andijan Provinces of Uzbekistan in April 2024 has signified a growing trend toward the institutionalization of interregional ties and CBC between the two nations (Gazeta.uz 2024).

Building on its ongoing *efforts to strengthen regional connectivity*, Uzbekistan has taken a significant step forward in enhancing cross-border trade and economic cooperation with neighboring countries by planning to establish trade-logistical zones along its borders. One example is the agreement between Uzbekistan and Kazakhstan to create a free trade zone, the International Center for Industrial Cooperation "Central Asia" (to be discussed in more detail in the following section) on their shared border. The agreement regulating its operations was signed in November 2023. On August 6, 2024, the Uzbek president signed a decree to formally establish this special economic zone in the Syrdarya region, covering an area of 50 hectares, which represented a concrete step toward implementing this initiative (Lex.uz 2024).

Regarding Uzbek–Turkmen cooperation, in 2022 the two countries signed an agreement to establish the "Shavat-Dashoguz" cross-border trade zone. In February 2024, President Mirziyoyev signed an order to initiate the project in the Khorezm region, moving the initiative into its implementation phase (NCa 2024). Plans are also underway to develop a similar trade zone at the border between Uzbekistan's Bukhara region and Turkmenistan's Lebap province.

The diplomatic thaw between Tashkent and Dushanbe has also rapidly translated into enhanced connectivity and trade. In 2018, eight road checkpoints were reopened, and the Galaba–Amuzang–Khushadi railway line, inactive for 20 years, was restored. Regular flights between Tashkent and Dushanbe resumed in 2021, followed by the launch of international bus routes such as "Samarkand–Dushanbe" and "Penjikent–Samarkand" in 2022. That same year, five new road routes, including "Tashkent–Khujand," and a passenger train service between Tashkent and Dushanbe were introduced. These efforts have had a transformative impact: between 2016 and 2023, rail freight volume between the two countries increased more than 25-fold, from 300,000 tons to 8.5 million tons, while road freight doubled to 1.5 million tons (Rahmatov 2024).

The evolving dynamics of the Tajik–Uzbek relationship have inevitably impacted their shared boundaries. Tajikistan's Sughd Region, Khatlon Region, and Tursunzoda District all border Uzbekistan. Remarkably, the Sughd Region has the most extensive interactions, as it hosts 12 of the 16 border crossings between the two nations. This region is adjacent to Uzbekistan's densely populated provinces—Jizzakh, Namangan, Samarkand, and Fergana, offering solid potential for robust cross-border exchanges.

It is therefore unsurprising that two new trade zones between the neighboring countries are planned along the border in the Sughd Region. The first is the Andarkhon Trade and Logistics Center, situated in Uzbekistan's Besharik District in the Fergana Region at the "Patar-Andarkhon" border crossing near Tajikistan's cities of Kanibadam and Isfara. The planned center, covering five hectares, began construction in March 2023 and aims to facilitate the exchange of goods between Uzbekistan's Fergana Region and Tajikistan's Sughd Region. It is designed to feature 200 retail outlets, a bank, dining facilities, a hotel, and a logistics hub, with the objective of promoting trade between enterprises from both regions (Khovar.tj 2023). This initiative is particularly notable given that the Patar border crossing—one of Tajikistan's major international gateways—was closed between 2009 and 2018 (Khovar.tj 2018).

The second initiative is the "Oybek-Fotekhobod Free Trade Zone," which was announced in 2022 and is planned to be established near the Fotekhobod border crossing in Tajikistan's Match District and the Oybek crossing in Uzbekistan's Bekabad District of the Tashkent Region (Spot.uz 2024b). Strategically located near Khujand, it serves as the closest checkpoint to Tashkent. The free trade zone is expected to include manufacturing enterprises as well as logistics and wholesale distribution infrastructure, thereby promoting economic growth and regional connectivity.

A similar initiative is under consideration with Kyrgyzstan. In 2022, Kyrgyz media reported plans to establish a trade-logistical center in Kara-Kiya on the Uzbekistan–Kyrgyzstan border, although this project has yet to materialize (Kapital.uz 2022).

Importantly, Uzbekistan's recently intensified cross-border contacts are supported by the establishment of new institutions and mechanisms. Uzbekistan has signed interregional memorandums, participated in interregional meetings, and created joint investment funds and companies with Kazakhstan, Kyrgyzstan, and Tajikistan. For instance, the Uzbek–Tajik Investment Company, established in 2021, oversees the implementation of cross-border trade zones (Spot.uz 2024b). In spring 2023, Uzbekistan and Kazakhstan established a joint company, Uzkaztrade, to facilitate bilateral trade (Spot.uz 2023). A year earlier, in 2022, Uzbekistan and Kyrgyzstan created a joint development fund with an initial capital of $50 million USD (Smekhova 2022).

3.3 Kazakhstan's Perspective

Kazakhstan is the second-largest country by area in post-Soviet Eurasia, after Russia. While geographically and politically belonging to Central Asia, it shares the world's longest continuous land border with Russia and a significant border with China. Although Kazakhstan's interaction with these two neighboring powers largely shapes

3.3 Kazakhstan's Perspective

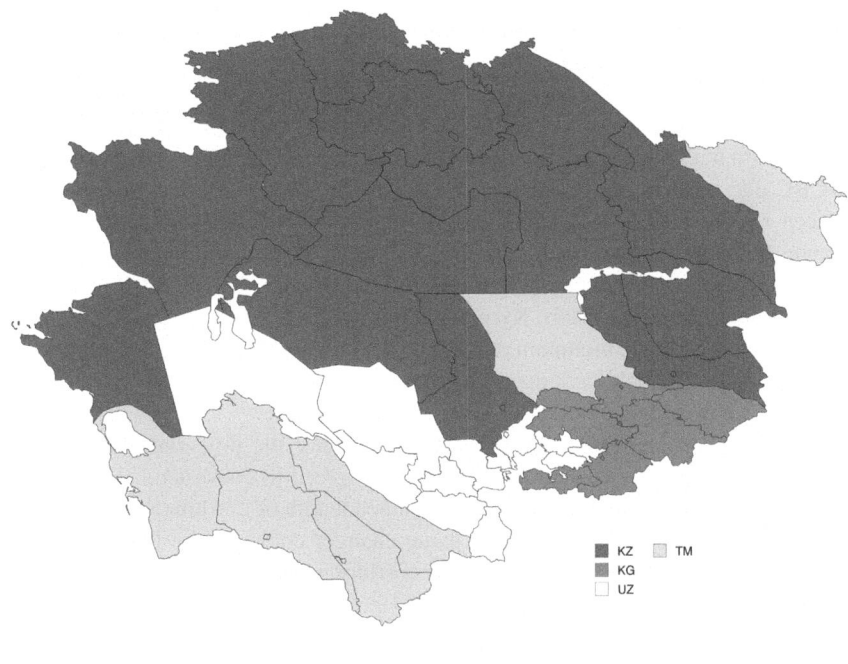

Fig. 3.5 Kazakhstan and neighboring Central Asian states

its national CBC policy, it typically plays the role of a policy-taker in these relationships. In contrast, Kazakhstan is more capable of playing a much more active policy-making role in its interactions with neighboring Central Asian states (Fig. 3.5).

Kazakhstan's neighboring countries in the region are not among its top economic partners: their combined share in Kazakhstan's trade turnover was around 1% in the early 2000s and approximately 5% in 2023 (Bureau of National Statistics of Kazakhstan n.d.; Observatory of Economic Complexity n.d.). For Uzbekistan and Kyrgyzstan, Kazakhstan's share is slightly higher but still below 10% (Internet Portal of the Commonwealth of Independent States 2024; National Statistical Committee of the Kyrgyz Republic n.d.). However, neighboring countries hold greater importance as trade partners for some Kazakh border regions. For instance, in 2020, Kyrgyzstan and Uzbekistan ranked second and third as export destinations for the Almaty region, accounting for some 20% each (QazIndustry 2022).

CBC and international regional cooperation receives some attention in Kazakhstan's framework and other agreements with neighboring Central Asian countries. For the most part, such cooperation is mentioned in passing, primarily as a declared intention to encourage collaboration between provinces, districts, and other administrative units, as well as contacts between the citizens of the two countries (Treaty on Strategic Partnership 2017).

Landscape, transport, and demographic proximities vary significantly across Kazakhstan's border territories. The westernmost regions—Mangystau, and especially Aktobe and Kyzylorda (the latter two lacking direct land transport links with neighboring countries)—account for approximately 45% of Kazakhstan's total border length with Central Asian states. These regions face significant disadvantages for CBC due to the sparse population of adjacent desert territories, the distances between major settlements in neighboring countries, and weak transport infrastructure. In the eastern part of Kazakhstan's Central Asian borderlands, despite the fact that the distance between the two-million-strong metropolis of Almaty and the region's primary summer resort, Kyrgyz Lake Issyk-Kul, is only 80 km in a straight line, natural barriers like mountain ranges and the absence of a direct road stretch the distance to 450 km, making cooperation between Almaty and the Issyk-Kul region much more challenging.

However, transport proximities in some areas have the potential to change in the future. In 2022, Kazakhstan and Kyrgyzstan agreed to construct a shorter road between Almaty and Cholpon-Ata, with a planned length of 279 km (Starkov 2024). For the Kyzylorda region, a potential game changer could be the long-discussed Kyzylorda–Uchkuduk railway and highway corridor project, first announced in 2021 but yet to reach implementation (Popova 2024).

The most significant proximities for Kazakhstan–Central Asia CBC do not always align with geographic proximity. Instead, they are primarily influenced by the mutual economic pull of major cities, the convenience of transportation links, and the overall economic potentials of neighboring economies. A key role is played by the economic and transport proximity between two major urban centers: 3-million-strong Tashkent and Shymkent, Kazakhstan's third-largest city with a population of 1.2 million, located just 125 km apart. In the Kazakhstan–Kyrgyzstan borderlands, the economic connection between Almaty and Bishkek is paramount, even though the transport distance between them is relatively long, spanning 235 km via a route passing through Kazakhstan's Almaty and Zhambyl regions and Kyrgyzstan's Chuy Region. Together, the Shymkent–Tashkent and Almaty–Bishkek proximities form the primary axes of Kazakhstan's CBC within Central Asia. Given that both axes traverse border regions, it is unsurprising that they account for the bulk of trade and business activity between these neighboring countries.

An important factor complementing these proximities is the policy of establishing cross-border logistical hubs. In 2019, the governments of Kazakhstan and Kyrgyzstan agreed to create a complex combining production and trade-logistics functions near the Karasu and Ak-Tilek border checkpoints. In 2023, this agreement was formalized (Government of the Republic of Kazakhstan 2023a), envisioning a facility spanning 7.6 square kilometers, focused on the production of dairy, fruit and vegetable, meat, textile, and pharmaceutical products. The necessity of completing this project was reiterated in a 2024 bilateral framework agreement (Akorda 2024).

3.3 Kazakhstan's Perspective

Similarly, in 2023, Kazakhstan and Uzbekistan signed an agreement to establish the "Central Asia" International Center for Industrial Cooperation, a one-square-kilometer complex at their border. This facility is designed to serve both logistical purposes and as a platform for joint industrial production, including by small enterprises from both countries (Government of the Republic of Kazakhstan 2023c).

These production-logistics complexes align with the economic proximities of Almaty–Bishkek and Tashkent–Shymkent, as they are located near key border checkpoints along major highways connecting these urban centers. However, the implementation of these projects has faced delays due to unresolved issues with investors and other challenges.

Kazakhstan's CBC with neighboring Central Asian countries is characterized by distinct features influenced by the nature of their political regimes, openness to international cooperation, economic capacities, geographical conditions, and other factors.

Relatively favorable political conditions for CBC have developed along the *Kazakhstan–Kyrgyzstan border*, the only Kazakhstan–Central Asian border where, due to the membership of both states in the Eurasian Economic Union, customs controls have been absent since 2015.

Unlike Kazakhstan's cross-border interactions with Uzbekistan and Turkmenistan, Kazakhstan–Kyrgyzstan regional contacts have faced fewer restrictions from central authorities since the early post-Soviet period. However, regional governments have also lacked the authority to enter into legally binding agreements. Several Kazakhstan–Kyrgyzstan agreements express interest in fostering regional and CBC. For instance, the 1997 treaty declares the intent to promote expanded interactions among residents of border areas (President of the Republic of Kazakhstan 1998), and the most recent 2024 framework agreement stipulates the annual convening of a Forum of Interregional Cooperation (Akorda 2024). Despite this formal framework, the first Kazakhstan–Kyrgyzstan interregional forum, during which contracts worth a relatively modest $60 million were signed, took place only in 2023 (Auelbekova 2023).

A key domain of Kazakhstan–Kyrgyzstan CBC is both formal and informal cross-border trade, including the development of logistics and transit routes through Kazakhstan between Kyrgyzstan and Russia. As early as the 2000s, Kazakhstan and Kyrgyzstan initiated the establishment of international cross-border cooperation centers "Aukhatty-Ken Bulun" and "Aysha Bibi-Chon Kapka," primarily aimed at addressing logistical challenges but also facilitating other cross-border interactions (Government of the Republic of Kazakhstan 2008). The effectiveness of these centers has been unfortunately limited by bureaucratic hurdles and frequent delays at the border due to periodic tightening of controls.

As noted earlier, in 2023, an agreement was signed to create a production and trade-logistics complex (spanning 7.6 sq. km and designed for producing dairy, fruit and vegetable, meat, textile, and pharmaceutical goods) near the "Karasu" and "Ak-Tilek" road checkpoints (Government of the Republic of Kazakhstan 2023c). However, the implementation of this agreement has been delayed, reportedly due to corruption-related challenges in identifying investors (Tusupbekova 2024).

Most projects aimed at creating new and developing existing transport corridors remain largely at the discussion stage. Some efforts are being made to foster cooperation between Almaty and Bishkek, including the development of a multifunctional corridor linking the two cities.

A cooperation agreement between the two metropolises was signed as early as November 1997 (Panorama 1997), and in November 2014, within the framework of the Central Asia Regional Economic Cooperation program, the authorities of both cities signed a memorandum on developing an economic corridor. This initiative aimed to create jobs, diversify the economy, and promote the sustainable development of both cities (Pestriakova 2014). The outcomes of this project, funded by the Asian Development Bank and implemented in 2017–2022, proved to be modest (Rosbach 2023); yet the role of the two cities in the Kazakh–Kyrgyz CBC remains significant anyway. For instance, in 2019, Almaty accounted for approximately 27% of Kazakhstan's external trade with Kyrgyzstan (Kazakh Invest n.d.). As mentioned earlier, the project to construct a highway connecting Almaty with Lake Issyk-Kul remains at a preliminary stage, despite similar ideas being discussed as far back as the 1990s.

Another important area of cooperation is water management, particularly the regulation of the use of water resources and hydraulic infrastructure on the transboundary Chu and Talas rivers. A 2000 agreement stands out as unique in Central Asia, as it formalizes the principle of shared financial responsibility for the operation of water management facilities located in Kyrgyzstan (such as dams, reservoirs, and canals) (Government of the Republic of Kazakhstan 2002).

The relations between the two countries regarding the regulation of cross-border and transboundary issues are far from smooth. Disagreements over the management of transboundary flows and the consumption of water resources occasionally lead to stricter border controls and delays at crossing points. Overall, Kazakhstan–Kyrgyzstan cross-border interactions are marked by numerous minor conflicts, which are generally resolved through compromises.

In 1998, Kyrgyzstan joined the WTO, turning its territory into a transit hub for Chinese goods entering Kazakhstan. This development led to the spread of practices involving the illegal importation of Chinese goods across the Kyrgyz–Kazakh border, prompting Kazakhstan to tighten its border controls. Tensions over border regulations resurfaced during the mass unrest in Kyrgyzstan in April 2010, which resulted in a change of government. Kazakhstan responded by closing its border, fully lifting the restrictions only in July, a move that caused severe economic difficulties for Kyrgyzstan (Vesti.kz 2010). Another round of disagreements between Bishkek and Astana emerged after the Eurasian Economic Union (EAEU) Customs Union was launched in 2011 on the external borders of Belarus, Kazakhstan, and Russia. This again prompted Kazakhstan to implement stricter customs controls along its borders with Kyrgyzstan, leading to periodic border congestion and related disputes (Zakon.kz 2011). The situation eased with Kyrgyzstan's accession to the EAEU in 2015, which eliminated customs controls at the border.

However, congestion has continued sporadically due to overloaded border infrastructure (Skripnik 2017), suspicions by Kazakh authorities of underreporting the customs value of goods imported via China (Bekbasova 2017), false transit claims for Kyrgyz goods ostensibly destined for Russia but actually sold within Kazakhstan (Ortcom.kz 2019), and seasonal spikes in agricultural product shipments (Kapitanova 2024). Disputes over the allocation of water resources from shared rivers also arise periodically, though both sides typically seek to resolve differences through negotiations and compromise.

Uzbekistan is Kazakhstan's most economically attractive partner in the region, with the bulk of activity concentrated in the densely populated area (over 8 million residents) between Turkestan and Tashkent regions. This area includes the independent administrative entities of Shymkent and Tashkent and accounts for approximately two-thirds of Kazakhstan's total trade with neighboring Central Asian countries (Bureau of National Statistics of Kazakhstan n.d.).

Historically, the populations of these territories maintained close cross-border ties. Post-Soviet tightening of the Kazakhstan–Uzbekistan border regime and the construction of physical barriers have pushed some of these interactions into illegality, including thriving industrial goods smuggling and local facilitation of unauthorized crossings. In the 1990s, territorial disputes between the two countries complicated cross-border contacts but were resolved through delimitation agreements in 2001–2002.

Official interactions between the border regions—primarily South Kazakhstan (now Turkestan) and Tashkent—did occur but were relatively infrequent, unstable, and heavily influenced by the broader political climate. Still, during one period of warming relations in 2007, an official delegation from South Kazakhstan, including business representatives, visited Uzbekistan and signed a memorandum of bilateral cooperation with the Tashkent region (Kazakhstanskaya Pravda 2007). Another memorandum was signed during a subsequent visit by the South Kazakhstan delegation in 2013 (Dobrota 2013). That same year, Uzbekistan opened trade houses in Shymkent and Saryagash (CA-News 2013), and in 2014, a Kazakh-Uzbek business forum was held in Shymkent (Kazakhstanskaya Pravda 2014).

The situation changed cardinally after Shavkat Mirziyoyev assumed the presidency of Uzbekistan in 2016. He implemented reforms such as introducing free currency convertibility for the Uzbek sum, promoting regional cooperation with neighboring countries, and even proposing the creation of an Association of Heads of Border Regions of Central Asian Countries (Sultan 2018).

Already by 2017, Kazakhstan and Uzbekistan signed an agreement on interregional cooperation, which outlined mechanisms such as working groups, consultations, roadmaps, experience sharing, coordination of infrastructure planning, business events, support for contract negotiations, and mutual information exchange, although it did not explicitly define the powers of regional authorities (Government of the Republic of Kazakhstan 2017). That same year, several memorandums of cooperation between regions of the two countries were signed (Baimanov 2017). Since 2018, regular Kazakh–Uzbek interregional cooperation forums have been held, with four convened as of late 2024. In 2024, construction began on the Darbaz–Maktaaral railroad section in the Turkestan region, bypassing the congested Saryagash station.

Systematic efforts to enhance proximity between Shymkent and Tashkent have yet to be undertaken, although some sporadic steps in this direction have been made. In 2019, the Asian Development Bank and CAREC promoted the idea of establishing an economic corridor connecting Shymkent, Tashkent, and Khujand (Gazeta.uz 2019).

Amid the growing momentum of cross-border cooperation, the governments of Kazakhstan and Uzbekistan proposed in October 2016 the establishment of a trade zone along the border between the South Kazakhstan and Tashkent regions (Kursiv.kz 2016). By 2019, this proposal evolved into an agreement to create the Central Asia International Trade and Economic Cooperation Center (Baigarin 2019). However, by December 2021, construction had not yet begun, and during subsequent negotiations, a decision was made to shift the center's focus toward industrial collaboration (Kun.uz 2021). In 2023, Kazakhstan and Uzbekistan signed an agreement to establish the Central Asia International Center for Industrial Cooperation. Spanning an area of 1 square kilometer, the center is designed to serve as a logistics hub and a platform for joint production involving industrial enterprises, including small businesses, from both countries (Government of the Republic of Kazakhstan 2023b).

While the primary focus of cross-border cooperation between Kazakhstan and Uzbekistan is concentrated in the relatively narrow zone between the Turkestan and Tashkent regions, some activity also takes place under less favorable conditions in the western border area, particularly between Kazakhstan's Mangystau Region and Uzbekistan's Republic of Karakalpakstan. This cooperation is shaped by Mangystau Region's status as one of Kazakhstan's wealthiest areas, with its port serving as Uzbekistan's gateway to the Caspian Sea, while Mangystau itself relies significantly on imports of Uzbek fruit and vegetables. Despite its relatively unfavorable position for CBC—lacking direct land connections with its neighboring region—another western Kazakh region, Kyzylorda Oblysy, has played an important role since the 1990s in bilateral and multilateral international efforts to address the Aral Sea crisis and manage the Syr Darya River's water usage.

Kazakhstan–Uzbekistan cooperation in the western border area gained momentum in the late 2010s. In 2019, Uzbekistan opened a consulate in Aktau. Efforts have been made to modernize cross-border transport routes between Mangystau Region and Karakalpakstan, alongside an increase in tourism cooperation. Mangystau is being promoted as a resort destination, while Karakalpakstan is positioned as a hub for ethnographic tourism (Mangystau Media 2022b; Zhaik Press 2024).

A significant boost to ecological cooperation involving Kyzylorda Region came with the establishment of the Kazakhstan–Uzbekistan working group on saving the Aral Sea in 2018. The governments of both countries committed to intensifying and closely coordinating their efforts, including sharing innovative practices for planting saxaul and tamarisk on the dried lakebed (Kuandykov 2018). These efforts received recognition from the United Nations General Assembly, which declared the Aral Sea region a zone of ecological innovations and technologies in May 2021 (United Nations General Assembly 2021).

The toughest regime for cross-border contacts, exacerbated by the non-convertibility of the Turkmen manat, persists along the *Kazakhstan–Turkmenistan border.* This border will be discussed in greater detail in the following section on Turkmenistan's perspective.

Certain CBC projects in the western border areas of Central Asia have a trilateral dimension. In 2016, Kazakhstan, Kyrgyzstan, and Uzbekistan successfully collaborated to have the "Western Tien-Shan" designated as a UNESCO World Natural Heritage site. This site includes 11 sections across seven nature reserves located within the territories of all three countries (ACBK 2021). Since 2023, Kazakhstan, Uzbekistan, and Turkmenistan have been working together on conservation efforts in border-adjacent areas on the Ustyurt Plateau, aiming to establish a transboundary protected area by integrating reserves under the jurisdiction of each country and implementing cross-border environmental initiatives (Stepanova and Bekbaev 2024). These efforts bear similarities to transboundary conservation projects implemented in countries like the United States and Canada.

Kazakhstan's efforts to develop transportation and logistical infrastructure in the rapidly growing village of Beineu, the largest in the country with a population exceeding 50,000, are also directed toward both Uzbekistan and Turkmenistan. These include the reconstruction of a grain terminal, which is expected to enhance the village's role as a key logistical hub (Mangystau Regional Government 2024).

3.4 Turkmenistan's Perspective

Turkmenistan is one of the world's most closed countries and remains the least open nation in Central Asia, hindering the development of both CBC and wider regional cooperation. Since 1995, it has maintained a distinct foreign policy of permanent neutrality, officially recognized by the United Nations. The country shares land borders with two Central Asian states, Kazakhstan and Uzbekistan, as well as Iran and Afghanistan to the south. It also has a maritime border with the littoral states of the Caspian Sea. Notably, four out of five regions in Turkmenistan share an international border. Turkmenistan has long underutilized its geographic potential and kept its insular stance. Only recently, the Turkmen government has shown signs for recognizing the need for greater cooperation with the outside world including along the border.

Turkmenistan and Kazakhstan share both a land border and a maritime boundary in the Caspian Sea. The Turkmen–Kazakh land border, spanning slightly over 450 km between Turkmenistan's Balkan province (*velayat*) and Kazakhstan's Mangystau region (*oblysy*), is the shortest state border for both countries. It primarily crosses sparsely populated desert areas, including the Ustyurt Plateau and regions near the Caspian Sea. This border was delimited in 2001 and demarcated in 2017, after which the two nations also defined their maritime boundary. In 2018, Turkmenistan and Kazakhstan, along with the other three Caspian littoral states, signed the Convention on the Legal Status of the Caspian Sea in Aktau. Later, in 2021, they signed an agreement on the delimitation of their maritime border and the division of fishing zones in the Caspian Sea (Government of the Republic of Kazakhstan 2022). In the

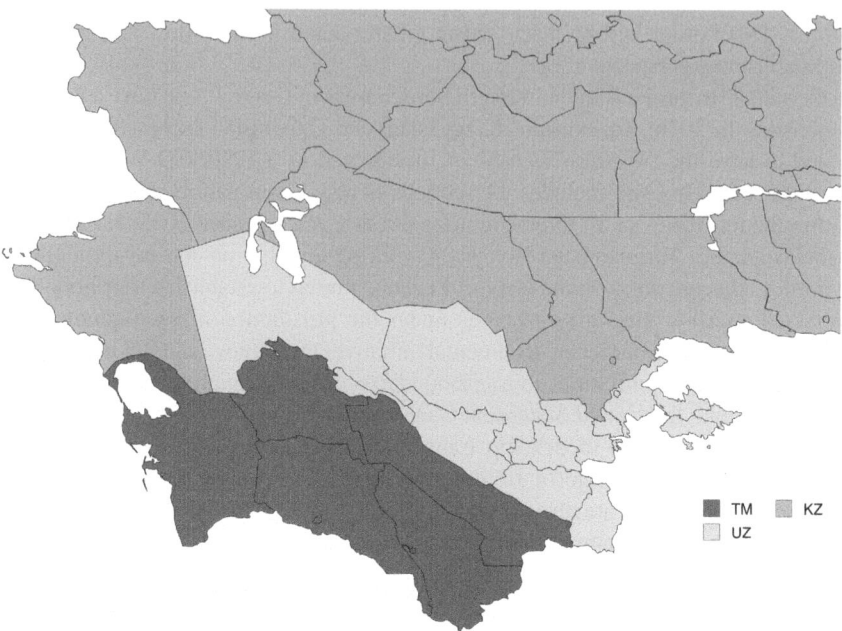

Fig. 3.6 Turkmenistan and neighboring Central Asian states

Caspian Sea, in addition to the Mangystau Region, Turkmenistan also shares a sea border with Kazakhstan's Atyrau Region (Fig. 3.6).

As previously noted, the borderlands between Turkmenistan and Kazakhstan are characterized by low population density. While the reliability of Turkmenistan's 2022 census remains in question, the data indicated that the Balkan Province, which also borders Iran to the south, is the least populated region in the country, accounting for only 7.5% of the country's total population. On the Kazakh side, the neighbouring Karakiya District, part of the Mangystau Region, had an estimated population of approximately 36,000 people as of 2023, demonstrating the sparsely inhabited nature of this transboundary area. Such low population density and the border area's perceived limited economic potential may partly explain Kazakhstan's historically limited proactivity in cross-border cooperation (CBC) with Turkmenistan.

Official cooperation between the regions of Turkmenistan and Kazakhstan remained minimal until the 2010s, although some industrial ties between enterprises in bordering regions have persisted since the dissolution of the Soviet Union. In May 2013, during a high-level meeting, Presidents Nursultan Nazarbayev and Gurbanguly Berdimuhamedow emphasized the importance of strengthening cooperation between Kazakhstan's Mangystau Region and Turkmenistan's Balkan Province, as well as supporting business forums (Vorotnoi 2013). As a result, consulates were established in the regional centers of Aktau and Turkmenbashi, a bilateral agreement on trade, economic, scientific, technical, and cultural cooperation was signed, and five-year cooperation plans were introduced.

3.4 Turkmenistan's Perspective

Since 2018, interregional business forums have been held, accompanied by a modest increase in official cultural exchanges. Discussions on establishing a Special Border Trade Zone have been ongoing since 2019 (Time.kz 2019), yet the project has faced significant delays with little tangible progress. In November 2023, during his visit to Kazakhstan, Gurbanguly Berdimuhamedov, Chairman of the Halk Maslahaty of Turkmenistan, reiterated the importance of creating a cross-border trade center to strengthen trade relations and increase mutual trade turnover to $1 billion. However, substantial progress toward its realization remains elusive.

In October 2024, Turkmenistan and Kazakhstan signed a Plan for Cooperation between the Administration of Balkan Province and the Akimat of Mangystau Region. The plan, targeting trade-economic, scientific-technical, and cultural collaboration through 2025, is intended to enhance the currently limited cross-border cooperation between the two countries. While the agreement's details remain unclear, its objectives reflect a commitment to addressing shared challenges (Moskovchiuk 2024).

The vernacular Kazakh–Turkmen CBC is significantly hindered by Turkmenistan's highly restrictive policies on the movement of people. As Turkmenistan enforces a visa regime for virtually all countries in the world, visas are required for travel between Turkmenistan and Kazakhstan. An exception is made for registered residents of the border regions—Balkan Province in Turkmenistan and the Mangystau and Atyrau Regions in Kazakhstan—who are allowed visa-free entry for up to five days, enabling limited local cross-border movement. These interactions typically revolve around visits to relatives and petty shuttle trade. Turkmen citizens often travel to Kazakhstan to purchase items in short supply at home, including US dollars, which are reportedly in high demand (Radiosy Azatlyk 2024). On their return, they bring permitted goods back to Turkmenistan, such as low-cost home appliances like vacuum cleaners and television sets. In addition, Kazakh cognac and cigarettes are popular commodities among Turkmen buyers. Conversely, Turkmen agricultural produce, including tomatoes and other fresh goods, finds a market on the Kazakh side (Toguzbaev 2017).

Many Turkmen citizens who travel to Kazakhstan on visas do so in search of employment opportunities. Considering Turkmenistan's challenging domestic conditions, including widespread unemployment, it is unsurprising that the flow of labor is predominantly one-sided, with Turkmen citizens seeking opportunities in Kazakhstan rather than the reverse. Additionally, a separate group, primarily ethnic Kazakhs, relocates to Kazakhstan on a permanent basis.

However, even this limited cross-border movement is often disrupted by unilateral border closures imposed by Turkmen authorities. This restrictive policy reflects the government's heightened sensitivity to outmigration and further limits the already minimal human-to-human cross-border interactions. Overall, transportation connectivity between the two countries remains limited. There is only one direct flight between Ashgabat and Almaty, which was suspended in March 2020 due to the COVID-19 pandemic and resumed three years later in March 2023. Turkmenistan's isolation, lack of connectivity, and stringent visa policies contribute to its perception as a "distant" country, with little appeal as a destination for Kazakh tourists.

Still, both Turkmenistan and Kazakhstan demonstrate a commitment to increasing the transborder connectivity both between the neighboring regions and as a part of wider international transportation corridors. Already in 2007, the project of the Ozen–Bereket–Gorgan railway route, which spans over 900 km and links Kazakhstan, Turkmenistan, and Iran, as part of the North–South Transport Corridor, was launched. Within this route, the longest segment, stretching 700 km, passes through Turkmenistan, highlighting the country's geographic centrality to the project. The project, that received financial assistance from the Asian Development Bank and the Islamic Development Bank, was completed in 2014 (Kayir and Bupezhanova 2014), contributing to improved cross-border connectivity and facilitating regional trade and cooperation. The Bolashak station, having special importance as a part of this route, was opened by Presidents Gurbanguly Berdymukhamedov and Nursultan Nazarbayev in May 2013 (Ospanova 2013). In 2024, government representatives of Turkmenistan, Kazakhstan, and Afghanistan convened in Aktau, Kazakhstan, to discuss plans for a new railway line connecting Turkmenistan and Afghanistan to Pakistan via Turgundi–Herat–Kandahar–Spin Buldak (News Central Asia 2024).

According to recent official data, Kazakh–Turkmen transportation has shown a consistent upward trend. In 2023, the volume of transported goods between the two countries increased by 20%, reaching 1.3 million tons. At the same time, bilateral trade volumes grew by 28%, amounting to $563 million. Over the past five years, mutual trade has nearly quadrupled, reflecting steady and modest growth in economic ties (Omirgazy 2024).

At present, there is only one automobile checkpoint crossing along the Turkmen-Kazakh border: the "Garabogaz" checkpoint on the Turkmen side and the "Temir Baba" checkpoint on the Kazakh side. Both Turkmenistan and Kazakhstan have expressed interest in enhancing the capacity of this checkpoint. In 2023, Kazakhstan initiated the reconstruction of Temir Baba (Mangystau Media 2022a), aiming for completion by the end of 2024. Similarly, Turkmenistan reported plans for the Garabogaz post to undergo reconstruction starting in 2024 (State Revenue Committee 2023).

Efforts to improve border efficiency include the adoption of digital systems by both nations. As of April 2024, the State Customs Service of Turkmenistan implemented the TIR-Electronic Pre-Declaration (TIR-EPD) system at all border checkpoints, including Garabogaz. This system aims to facilitate the faster movement of international cargo by allowing TIR Carnet holders to submit online pre-declarations to customs authorities (Golden Age 2024). In a similar move, Kazakhstan introduced an electronic queue system at its border checkpoints, including Temir Baba, in 2023 to streamline operations and reduce wait times (Business Turkmenistan 2023). Moreover, in October 2024, during President Tokayev's official visit to Turkmenistan, Kazakhstan and Turkmenistan signed a protocol amending their 1997 agreement on international road transport of passengers and cargo. This amendment abolished the requirement for permits for road cargo movement between the two countries, facilitating more efficient and streamlined trade (KazTAG 2024).

Kazakhstan and Turkmenistan are also developing cooperation in the Caspian Sea between Turkmenistan's Turkmenbashi port and Kazakhstan's ports of Aktau and

3.4 Turkmenistan's Perspective

Kuryk, while simultaneously competing for maritime cargo volumes. During President Tokayev's visit to Ashgabat, a Memorandum of Cooperation in Maritime Transport was signed between Turkmenistan's Marine Merchant Fleet and Kazakhstan's Aktau International Sea Commercial Port.

Kazakhstan and Turkmenistan are also developing cooperation in the Caspian Sea region, focusing on connections between Turkmenistan's port of Turkmenbashi and Kazakhstan's ports of Aktau and Kuryk, while simultaneously competing for maritime cargo volumes. In October 2024, during President Tokayev's visit to Ashgabat, a Memorandum of Cooperation in Maritime Transport was signed between Turkmenistan's Marine Merchant Fleet and Kazakhstan's Aktau International Sea Commercial Port (Akorda.kz 2024).

Turkmenistan's CBC with Uzbekistan is more dynamic and diverse, which can be explained both by more favorable conditions for cross-border cooperation specifically between Turkmenistan and Uzbekistan, as well as by Uzbekistan's more active and purposeful policy in establishing cross-border cooperation with its neighbors. Not only is the common state border long, at 1650 km, but the shared border regions are densely populated. For instance, two major Turkmen cities, Turkmenabad and Dashoguz, are located in close proximity to Uzbekistan, presenting a different demographic dynamic compared to the cross-border ties between Turkmenistan and Kazakhstan. Notably, while Turkmenistan is believed to host approximately 300,000 ethnic Uzbeks, Uzbekistan is home to around 200,000 ethnic Turkmens (Akhal-Teke 2023).

Turkmenistan's Dashoguz Province (*velayat*) and Lebap Province share land borders with Uzbekistan's Karakalpakstan Republic, Khorezm Region, and Bukhara Region, respectively. The Turkmen–Uzbek border was delimited in 2019, and although its demarcation is still ongoing, the process appears to be progressing smoothly without major challenges. The Amu Darya River, which traverses both countries, plays a vital role in shared water and energy management across the border regions. In this context, the establishment of a Turkmen-Uzbek Intergovernmental Commission on Water Management Issues in May 2021 marks an important institutional development. The commission held its first meeting in September 2021 in Tashkent, followed by the second in July 2022 in Dashoguz, and the latest, fourth, meeting in April 2024 in Turkmenabad. A notable outcome of this collaboration was the signing of a bilateral agreement in July 2022 on the management, protection, and rational use of the Amu Darya River's water resources. This agreement aims to enhance water management on the Turkmen–Uzbek section of the river.

A key infrastructure in this cooperation is the Tuyamuyun Hydro Complex (THC), located downstream along the Amu Darya. The THC regulates the river's flow and oversees the distribution of water and energy resources between Uzbekistan and Turkmenistan. It supports irrigation for 779,300 hectares of farmland in Uzbekistan and 425,000 hectares in Turkmenistan, generates 450 million kWh of electricity annually for Uzbekistan, and supplies drinking water to the Khorezm Region and Karakalpakstan. It is worth noting that the THC is a significant project within the EU-funded "Central Asia Nexus Dialogue Project: Fostering Water, Energy, and Food Security Nexus and Multi-Sector Investment" (NEXUS) program (CAREC 2022).

Systematic contacts between the border regions of Turkmenistan and Uzbekistan began to develop in 2018, when a business forum was held under the auspices of the administrations of the Lebap Region of Turkmenistan and the Bukhara Region of Uzbekistan. The First Turkmen-Uzbek Interregional Forum was held in Bukhara in 2022, resulting, among other things, in the signing of business agreements totaling $451 million and the adoption of a project to create a cross-border trade center near the city of Dashoguz (Orient 2022), which is currently under construction. The second Turkmen–Uzbek Interregional Forum was held in 2024 in Turkmenabat, where participants discussed the expansion of cross-border trade, the development of transport and logistics infrastructure, and the strengthening of cultural and humanitarian ties between the two countries (Türkmen Döwlet Habarlary 2024).

3.5 Kyrgyzstan's and Tajikistan's Perspectives

As previously mentioned, a significant challenge in structuring this chapter is avoiding duplication in the analysis of individual border situations if the perspectives of all Central Asian countries are examined in detail. Cross-border cooperation along most Central Asian borders has already been reviewed, leaving only the situation on the Kyrgyz–Tajik border unaddressed. Considering this, we find it appropriate to combine the analysis of Kyrgyzstan's and Tajikistan's perspectives into a single section.

Kyrgyzstan and Tajikistan, located in the southern part of Central Asia, are landlocked, mountainous, and upstream countries. The Kyrgyz population is some 7 million while the Tajik population is around 10 million. Economically, both countries remain underdeveloped. Tajikistan has the lowest GDP per capita in Central Asia, recorded at USD 1,12 thousand in 2023, while Kyrgyzstan's GPD was USD 1,97 thousand (World Bank 2024). It is important to note that Tajikistan's economy and overall development have been significantly affected by the civil war from 1992 to 1997 (Malashenko 2012).

Tajikistan is governed by a highly centralized authoritarian regime, ranking second only to Turkmenistan in terms of political control. Kyrgyzstan, despite its declining democracy ranking and current classification as a "consolidated authoritarian regime" by Freedom House, still holds the highest democracy score among the five Central Asian states (Freedom House 2024).

Culturally, Tajikistan's uniqueness lies in its language: It is the only Central Asian country where the majority speaks Tajik, a variety of Persian and a non-Turkic language, although, as elsewhere in the region, bilingulism or multilingualism is a common trait. The majority of Kyrgyzstan's population speak Kyrgyz, which is a Turkic language, while Russian is also widespread.

Tajikistan shares a border of approximately 1330 km with Uzbekistan to the northwest and about 980 km with Kyrgyzstan to the northeast. To the south, Tajikistan has a lengthy border of nearly 1380 km with Afghanistan, much of which follows the Amu Darya River. Its eastern border with China, stretching approximately 500 km,

3.5 Kyrgyzstan's and Tajikistan's Perspectives

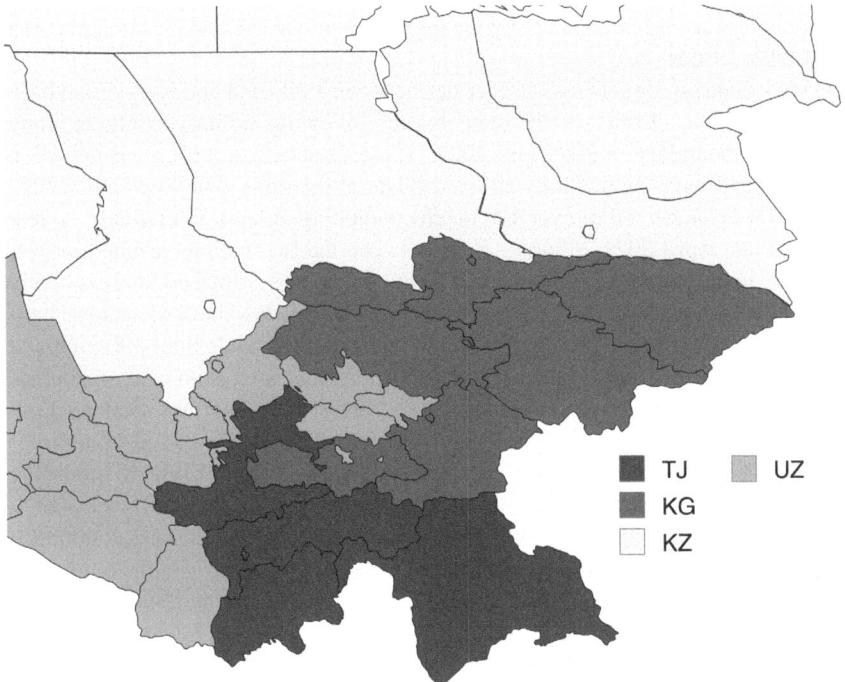

Fig. 3.7 Kyrgyzstan, Tajikistan, and the neighboring Central Asian states

runs along the rugged Pamir Mountains (Ministry of Foreign Affairs of the Republic of Tajikistan 2013). The combination of these characteristics significantly influences Tajikistan's cross-border interactions and its role within the broader dynamics of Central Asia. Like Tajikistan, Kyrgyzstan borders Uzbekistan (1378 km) and China (1034 km). It also borders Kazakhstan (1242 km) (Fig. 3.7).

The economic weakness and limited resources of Kyrgyzstan and Tajikistan reduce their ability to independently initiate cross-border cooperation (CBC) projects, largely positioning them as policy-takers in Central Asian CBC. At the same time, Kyrgyzstan is one of the most open countries in the region to various forms of cooperation, with regional authorities being relatively less restrictive in developing international contacts. Additionally, it boasts one of the most attractive recreational potentials in the region, primarily due to Lake Issyk-Kul and its established infrastructure. Tajikistan, being a more authoritarian state, still responds positively to cross-border cooperation initiatives from wealthier Uzbekistan and to transboundary projects initiated by international organizations for the development of the Fergana Valley. These include the above-mentioned projects aimed at fostering reconciliation between Tajik and Kyrgyz communities in the Isfara Valley.

As discussed earlier, the previously strained relations between Uzbekistan and its neighbors Kyrgyzstan and Tajikistan have significantly improved since Mirziyoyev's ascession to power in Uzbekistan. The two neighbors are now experiencing a diplomatic honeymoon, marked by the reopening of borders and the strengthening of cross-border ties.

In stark contrast, direct cross-border ties between Tajikistan and Kyrgyzstan have halted due to the closure of the state border following military conflicts along their shared boundary in 2021 and 2022. These clashes resulted in casualties on both sides and have significantly strained bilateral relations. The September 2022 conflict, for instance, led to over 100 deaths, including at least 37 civilians. A year earlier, in late April 2021, a border clash between the two nations resulted in over 50 deaths, mainly among civilians, injured hundreds, and displaced approximately 58,000 people (Sultanalieva 2022). Similar border skirmishes (but less violent) have continuously occurred in the Fergana Valley, where Tajikistan's Sughd Region and Kyrgyzstan's Batken Region meet. This densely populated area, with scarce resources such as water, has seen frequent disputes. The biggest flashpoint has been the Tajik exclave of Vorukh, surrounded by Kyrgyz territory. With a population of approximately 40,000, resolving the issues surrounding Vorukh remains difficult, unlike the situation with the aforementioned Barak, a former Kyrgyz exclave in Uzbekistan.

Despite these challenges, recent developments suggest that both states continue to engage in border negotiations. According to the latest reports, 93% of the border has been demarcated, indicating progress in addressing long-standing issues. However, the remaining disputes in the Fergana Valley continue to be a source of friction. While the border in the Fergana Valley has been contentious, the border between Kyrgyzstan's Osh Region and Tajikistan's Murgab District in the Gorno-Badakhshan Autonomous Region (GBAO) has remained peaceful. The closure of the border, however, has disrupted movement and trade in this historically connected region. Murgab, where approximately 70% of residents are ethnic Kyrgyz, has traditionally maintained close social ties with Osh. The severed connections have adversely affected these ties, including shortages of foods and goods in Murgab, which shows well the socio-economic costs of the border disputes (Pamir Inside 2021). Interestingly, during Tajikistan's civil war, the Osh–Murgab border crossing served as a crucial gateway for delivering humanitarian aid to GBAO.

Further intensification and institutionalization of CBC could potentially evolve into a multilateral CBC framework. Notably, in April 2021, the governors of three bordering regions—Fergana in Uzbekistan, Sughd in Tajikistan, and Batken in Kyrgyzstan—met in Fergana to discuss ways to strengthen ties among the border regions of their respective countries. During his speech, Rajabboy Ahmadzoda expressed the Sughd Region's commitment to advancing investment and joint projects. The forum concluded with the signing of a Memorandum of Cooperation between the Sughd and Fergana regions, as well as agreements between the cities and districts of Kanibadam and Besharik, Guliston and Buvayda, Bobojon Gafurov and Dangara, Isfara and Uzbekistan, and Buston and Uchkuprik (Kabar.kg 2021). However, cooperation among the Fergana Valley regions has primarily continued in the bilateral Tajik–Uzbek format. These developments underscore the potential for regional collaboration in the Fergana Valley, offering hope that even the more challenging areas of cross-border cooperation, such as the Kyrgyz–Tajik border, may see progress in the future.

3.6 Conclusion

Compared to other regions of the world, the conditions for CBC in Central Asia can be described as mixed.

On the one hand, such cooperation is facilitated by the regional integration agenda, the aspiration of countries to overcome geographical isolation, intensive transport connections between major urban centers, and vibrant informal cross-border trade in some areas of the region. A significant positive factor has been the notable intensification of Uzbekistan's regional cooperation policies after 2016. Uzbekistan, as the core country of the region and the only one bordering all other Central Asian states, has played a pivotal role in fostering collaboration among its neighbors. On the other hand, CBC in the region faces obstacles such as the dominance of authoritarian centralized governance, limited financial resources, challenging geographical conditions in the western and eastern parts of the region, and high levels of corruption.

While the mentioned factors are fairly typical in a global context, they necessitate careful consideration in devising regional CBC strategies that adequately account for local specificities.

References

ACBK. 2021. UNESCO Heritage [in Russian]. Association for the Conservation of Biodiversity of Kazakhstan. March 31. https://www.acbk.kz/article/default/view?id=13.

Akhal-Teke. 2023. Turkmenistan: Uzbek to the Future. *Eurasianet*. September 5. https://eurasianet.org/turkmenistan-uzbek-to-the-future.

Akorda. 2021. Joint statement following the consultative meeting [in Kazakh]. *Akorda.kz*. https://www.akorda.kz/kz/konsultativtik-kezdesuinin-korytyndysy-boyynsha-birlesken-malimdeme-67933.

Akorda. 2024. Kassym-Jomart Tokayev and Sadyr Japarov held a briefing for media representatives [in Kazakh]. *Akorda.kz*. April 19. https://www.akorda.kz/kz/kasym-zhomart-tokaev-pen-sadyr-zhaparov-bak-okilderi-ushin-brifing-otkizdi-193822.

Aminjonov, Farkhod. 2016. Central Asian Countries' power systems are now isolated, but not everyone is happy! 2016. https://www.eurasian-research.org/publication/central-asian-countries-power-systems-are-now-isolated-but-not-everyone-is-happy/.

Asian Development Bank. 2020. *Strengthening cross-border community collaboration in the CAREC region: A scoping study*, 0 ed. Manila, Philippines: Asian Development Bank. https://doi.org/10.22617/TCS200414-2.

Auelbekova, Aizhan. 2023. A new impulse to eternal relations [in Russian]. Vremya. September 25. https://time.kz/articles/zloba/2023/09/25/novyj-impuls-vechnym-otnosheniyam.

Boyarov, Aziz. 2024. Turkmenistan and Uzbekistan Will Hold an Intergovernmental Commission Meeting on the Demarcation of Their Common Border [in Russian]. Daryo, April 9. https://daryo.uz/ru/2024/04/09/turkmenistan-i-uzbekistan-provedut-zasedanie-mezpravkomissii-po-demarkacii-obsej-granicy.

Baigarin, Meirambek. 2019. International trade center to be built on the Kazakhstan-Uzbekistan border [in Russian]. Zakon.kz. April 29. https://online.zakon.kz/Document/?doc_id=32139550.

Baimanov, Damir. 2017. Expert: Regions of Kazakhstan and Uzbekistan strengthen cross-border cooperation [in Russian]. Zakon.Kz. September 18. https://www.zakon.kz/redaktsiia-zakonkz/4878599-ekspert-regiony-kazakhstana-i.html.

Bekbasova, Anar. 2017. Kazakhstan may tighten control on the border with Kyrgyzstan [in Russian]. Ratel.kz. November 2. https://ratel.kz/raw/kazahstan_mozhet_usilit_kontrol_na_granitse_s_kyrgyzstanom?page=1.

BOMCA. n.d. Background. BOMCA. https://www.bomca-eu.org/en/what-we-do/background. Accessed 2 Dec 2024.

Buranelli, Filippo Costa. 2021. Central Asian Regionalism or Central Asian order? Some reflections. *Central Asian Affairs* 8 (1): 1–26. https://doi.org/10.30965/22142290-bja10015.

Bureau of National Statistics of Kazakhstan. n.d. Key indicators of foreign trade by country [in Russian]. Bureau of National Statistics of Kazakhstan. https://stat.gov.kz/api/iblock/element/60181/file/ru/.

Business Turkmenistan. 2023. Kazakhstan to Introduce electronic queue on border with Turkmenistan | Regional. Business Turkmenistan Information Center. February 17. https://business.com.tm/post/9859/kazakhstan-to-introduce-electronic-queue-on-border-with-turkmenistan.

CABAR.asia. 2021. How are negotiations on the border between Tajikistan and Uzbekistan being conducted? *CABAR.Asia* (blog). June 21. https://cabar.asia/en/?p=46356.

CABAR.asia. 2023. Kyrgyzstan: Authorities are delaying the Kempir-Abad Case. February 7. https://cabar.asia/ru/kyrgyzstan-vlasti-zatyagivayut-delo-po-kempir-abadu.

CA-News. 2013. Uzbek trade house opened in Kazakhstan [in Russian]. *Ca-News.Org*, December 19. Retrieved via Integrum World Wide database.

CAREC. 2022. Transboundary Nexus demo project between Uzbekistan and Turkmenistan 'Tuyamuyun Hydroelectric Complex.' CAREC. September 9. https://carececo.org/en/main/news/news/transgranichnyy-neksus-demo-proekt-mezhdu-uzbekistanom-i-turkmenistanom-tuyamuyunskiy-gidrouzel/?utm_source=chatgpt.com.

carececo.org. 2022. Transboundary Nexus demo project between Uzbekistan and Turkmenistan 'Tuyamuyun Hydroelectric Complex.' Carececo.Org. September 9. https://carececo.org/en/main/news/news/transgranichnyy-neksus-demo-proekt-mezhdu-uzbekistanom-i-turkmenistanom-tuyamuyunskiy-gidrouzel/?utm_source=chatgpt.com.

Chorshanbiev, Pairav. 2023. Tajik-Uzbek strategic partnership is 5 years old. What has changed? | Tajikistan News ASIA-Plus. August 17. https://asiaplustj.info/en/news/tajikistan/politics/20230817/tajik-uzbek-strategic-partnership-is-5-years-old-what-has-changed?utm_source=chatgpt.com.

Collins, Kathleen. 2009. Economic and security regionalism among patrimonial authoritarian regimes: The case of Central Asia. *Europe-Asia Studies* 61 (2): 249–281.

Dadabaev, Timur. 2019. Uzbekistan as Central Asian game changer? Uzbekistan's foreign policy construction in the Post-Karimov Era. *Asian Journal of Comparative Politics* 4 (2): 162–175. https://doi.org/10.1177/2057891118775289.

Dobrota, Liubov. 2013. Neighbors signed a memorandum [in Russian]. *Kazakhstanskaya Pravda*, November 6.

Eurasianet. 2022a. Uzbekistan commits to buying power from Tajikistan's Roghun Plant. Eurasianet. June 3. https://eurasianet.org/uzbekistan-commits-to-buying-power-from-tajikistans-roghun-plant.

Eurasianet. 2022b. Uzbekistan: Russia reclaims top trading partner position from China | Eurasianet. Eurasianet. January 24. https://eurasianet.org/uzbekistan-russia-reclaims-top-trading-partner-position-from-china.

FAO. 2023. FAO country profiles | support to rural people in border regions of Kyrgyzstan and Uzbekistan lifts prosperity. FAO. August 25. https://www.fao.org/countryprofiles/news-archive/detail-news/en/c/1649220.

Finke, Peter, and Meltem Sancak. 2012. To be an Uzbek or not to be a Tajik? Ethnicity and locality in the Bukhara Oasis. *Zeitschrift Für Ethnologie* 137 (1): 47–70.

Freedom House. 2024. Countries and territories. Freedom House. 2024. https://freedomhouse.org/countries/nations-transit/scores.

Gazeta.uz. 2019. ADB proposed creating a new corridor for the integration of Central Asian Countries [in Russian]. Gazeta.Uz. May 31. https://www.gazeta.uz/ru/2019/05/31/corridor/.

References

gazeta.uz. 2024. Uzbekistan and Tajikistan sign treaty on allied relations. Gazeta.Uz. April 18. https://www.gazeta.uz/en/2024/04/18/agreements/.

genevawaterhub.org. 2020. Hydrodiplomacy in rapid action: Early insights from the Sardoba Dam disaster in Central Asia | Geneva Water Hub. Genevawaterhub.org. September 9. https://www.genevawaterhub.org/news/hydrodiplomacy-rapid-action-early-insights-sardoba-dam-disaster-central-asia?utm_source=chatgpt.com.

Golden Age. 2024. TIR-EPD information system introduced in Turkmenistan. Electronic Newspaper «Golden Age». April 3. https://turkmenistan.gov.tm/en/post/82178/tir-epd-information-system-introduced-turkmenistan.

Government of the Republic of Kazakhstan. 2002. On the ratification of the agreement between the government of the Republic of Kazakhstan and the Government of the Kyrgyz Republic on the use of interstate water facilities on the Chu and Talas Rivers [in Kazakh]. https://adilet.zan.kz/kaz/docs/Z020000301_.

Government of the Republic of Kazakhstan. 2008. On the approval of the framework agreement between the Government of the Republic of Kazakhstan and the Government of the Kyrgyz Republic on the Establishment of the international cross-border cooperation centers 'Aukhatty—Ken-Bulun' and 'Aysha Bibi—Chong-Kapka' [in Kazakh]. Adilet. https://adilet.zan.kz/kaz/docs/P080000122_.

Government of the Republic of Kazakhstan. 2017. On the approval of the agreement between the Government of the Republic of Kazakhstan and the Government of the Republic of Uzbekistan on interregional cooperation [in Kazakh]. Adilet. https://adilet.zan.kz/kaz/docs/P1700000416.

Government of the Republic of Kazakhstan. 2022. Law of the Republic of Kazakhstan on the ratification of the treaty between the Republic of Kazakhstan and Turkmenistan on the Delimitation of the State Border in the Caspian Sea and the Division of Adjacent Fishing Zones [in Kazakh]. https://adilet.zan.kz/rus/docs/Z2200000150.

Government of the Republic of Kazakhstan. 2023a. On the signing of the agreement between the Government of the Republic of Kazakhstan and the Cabinet of Ministers of the Kyrgyz Republic on Regulating the activities of the industrial trade and logistics complex near the 'Karasu' and 'Ak-Tilek' Border Checkpoints [in Kazakh]. Adilet. https://adilet.zan.kz/kaz/docs/P2300000423.

Government of the Republic of Kazakhstan. 2023b. On the signing of the agreement between the Government of the Republic of Kazakhstan and the Government of the Republic of Uzbekistan on Regulating the activities of the 'Central Asia' International Center for industrial cooperation [in Kazakh]. Adilet. https://adilet.zan.kz/kaz/docs/P2300000680.

Government of the Republic of Kazakhstan. 2023c. On the signing of the agreement between the Government of the Republic of Kazakhstan and the Government of the Republic of Uzbekistan on regulating the activities of the international center for industrial cooperation 'Central Asia' [in Kazakh]. Adilet. https://adilet.zan.kz/kaz/docs/P2300000680.

Kabar.kg. 2021. The Fergana meeting of regional governors from three countries discussed cooperation issues. kabar.kg. April 23. https://kabar.kg/news/ferganskaia-vstrecha-glav-oblastei-trekh-stran-regiona-rassmotrela-voprosy-sotrudnichestva/.

Kaminski, Bartlomiej, and Saumya Mitra. 2012. *Borderless bazaars and regional integration in Central Asia: Emerging patterns of trade and cross-border cooperation.* Washington, DC: The World Bank.

kapital.uz. 2022. Kyrgyzstan to become a transit corridor between Uzbekistan and China. Kapital.uz. April 14. https://kapital.uz/kyrgyzstan-uzb-china/.

Kapitanova, Irina. 2024. Kyrgyzstan wants to increase the number of checkpoints on the border with Kazakhstan [in Russian]. Zakon.kz. October 16. https://www.zakon.kz/mir/6452607-kyrgyzstan-khochet-uvelichit-kolichestvo-kpp-na-granitse-s-kazakhstanom.html.

Kayir, Azamat, and Danna Bupezhanova. 2014. Nazarbayev helps launch last section of Kazakhstan-Turkmenistan-Iran railway. *The Astana Times.* December 4. https://astanatimes.com/2014/12/nazarbayev-helps-launch-last-section-kazakhstan-turkmenistan-iran-railway/.

Kazakh Invest. n.d. Markets. *Kazakh Invest.* https://almaty.invest.gov.kz/about/markets/. Accessed 1 Dec 2024.

Kazakhstanskaya Pravda. 2014. The basis of cross-border partnership [in Russian]. *Kazakhstanskaya Pravda*, March 19.

Kazakhstanskaya Pravda. 2007. Joint border and common interest [in Russian]. *Kazakhstanskaya Pravda*, May 18.

KazTAG. 2024. Declaration on strengthening friendship and partnership between Kazakhstan and Turkmenistan adopted [in Russian]. *KazTAG.* October 10. https://kaztag.kz/ru/news/prinyata-deklaratsiya-ob-ukreplenii-druzhby-partnerstva-mezhdu-kazakhstanom-i-turkmenistanom.

Khovar.tj. 2018. After a long hiatus, the 'Andarkhon-Patar' checkpoint reopens. *Khovar.tj.* February 13. https://khovar.tj/rus/2018/02/posle-dolgogo-pereryva-vnov-otkrylsya-kontrolno-propusknoj-punkt-andarhon-patar/.

Khovar.tj. 2023. Foundation stone laid for 'Andarkhon' Trade and Logistics Center at the Tajikistan-Uzbekistan border. *Khovar.tj.* March 14. https://khovar.tj/rus/2023/03/na-granitse-tadzhikistana-i-uzbekistana-zalozhen-kamen-v-fundament-dlya-sozdaniya-torgovo-logicheskogo-tsentra-andarhon/.

Kuandykov, Miras. 2018. Kazakhstan and Uzbekistan to create a working group to save the Aral Sea [in Russian]. Kazinform. March 2. https://www.inform.kz/ru/kazahstan-i-uzbekistan-sozdadut-rabochuyu-gruppu-po-spaseniyu-arala_a3171245.

Kudryavtseva, Tatyana. 2017. Kyrgyzstan and Uzbekistan agree on Kambarata and Kasansay Reservoir—24.Kg. October 6. https://24.kg/english/64767_Kyrgyzstan_and_Uzbekistan_agree_on_Kambarata_and_Kasansay_reservoir/.

Kun.uz. 2021. Future international center on the Uzbekistan-Kazakhstan border changes its focus [in Russian]. Kun.uz. December 29. https://kun.uz/ru/news/2021/12/29/budushchiy-mejdunarodnyy-sentr-na-granitse-uzbekistana-i-kazaxstana-smenil-svoye-napravleniye.

Kursiv.kz. 2016. Kazakhstan and Uzbekistan plan to create a trade zone [in Russian]. Kursiv.Kz. October 11. https://kz.kursiv.media/2016-10-11/kazakhstan-i-uzbekistan-planiruyut-sozdanie-torgovoy-zony/.

Laumulin, Murat. 2018. The current political development and international position of 'Post-Karimov' Uzbekistan (the view of Western experts). International Science Complex Astana. December 24. http://isca.kz/en/pubs-en/analytics-en/3034.

lex.uz. 2024. Decree of the President of the Republic of Uzbekistan on the establishment of the free economic zone 'Central Asia International Center for Industrial Cooperation' (in Russian). Lex.Uz. August 6. https://lex.uz/ru/pdfs/7050365.

Malashenko, Alexey. 2012. Tajikistan: Civil War's long echo. Carnegie Moscow Center. https://www.jstor.org/stable/resrep26714.

Mangystau Regional Government. 2024. A 100,000-ton grain terminal to be opened in Mangystau [in Kazakh]. Government of Kazakhstan. May 6. https://www.gov.kz/memleket/entities/mangystau/press/news/details/766499?lang=kk.

Mangystau Media. 2022a. Kazakhstan and Turkmenistan to be connected by a bridge across the bay [in Russian]. Mangystau Media. August 9. https://mangystaumedia.kz/ru/region/115621.

Mangystau Media. 2022b. Tourism development with Karakalpakstan discussed in Mangystau [in Russian]. Mangystau Media. November 27. https://mail.7292info.kz/ru/region/v_mangistau_obsudili_razvitie_turizma_s_karakalpakstanom.

Megoran, Nick. 2017. *Nationalism in Central Asia: A Biography of the Uzbekistan-Kyrgyzstan boundary.* Pittsburgh: University of Pittsburgh Press. https://muse.jhu.edu/pub/49/monograph/book/55767.

Ministry of foreign affairs of the Republic of Tajikistan. 2013. Tajikistan and Uzbekistan State Boundary. Ministry of Foreign Affairs of the Republic of Tajikistan. March 1. https://mfa.tj/en/main/view/152/tajik-uzbek-state-border.

Minority Rights Group. 2018. Uzbeks in Tajikistan. Minority Rights Group. April 2018. https://minorityrights.org/communities/uzbeks-3/.

References

Mirziyoyev, Shavkat. 2017. Address by H.E. Mr. Shavkat Mirziyoyev, the President of the Republic of Uzbekistan at the UNGA-72 | Uzbekistan. The Permanent Mission of the Republic of Uzbekistan to the United Nations. 2017. https://www.un.int/uzbekistan/statements_speeches/address-he-mr-shavkat-mirziyoyev-president-republic-uzbekistan-unga-72.

Moldashev, Kairat, and Ikboljon Qoraboyev. 2018. From regional integration to soft institutionalism: What kind of regionalism for Central Asia? SSRN Scholarly Paper. Rochester, NY: Social Science Research Network. https://doi.org/10.2139/ssrn.3320307.

Moskovchiuk, Anastasia. 2024. What documents were signed by Kazakhstan and Turkmenistan. Zakon.kz. October 10. https://www.zakon.kz/politika/6451917-kakie-dokumenty-podpisali-kaz akhstan-i-turkmenistan.html.

Mukhammadiev, Bakhtiyor. 2014. Challenges of transboundary water resources management in Central Asia. In *The Aral Sea: The devastation and partial rehabilitation of a Great Lake*, edited by Philip Micklin, N.V. Aladin, and Igor Plotnikov, 233–251. Berlin, Heidelberg: Springer. https://doi.org/10.1007/978-3-642-02356-9_9.

National Statistical Committee of the Kyrgyz Republic. n.d. Foreign Economic activity statistics [in Russian]. National Statistical Committee of the Kyrgyz Republic. https://stat.gov.kg/en/sta tistics/vneshneekonomicheskaya-deyatelnost/.

nCa. 2024. President of Uzbekistan signs decree on establishing the 'Uzbekistan–Turkmenistan' free trade zone. *News Central Asia (nCa)* (blog). March 1. https://www.newscentralasia.net/2024/03/01/prezident-uzbekistana-podpisal-postanovleniye-o-sozdanii-zony-svobodnoy-tor govli-uzbekistan-turkmenistan/.

News Central Asia. 2024. Turkmenistan, Kazakhstan, Afghanistan enhance transport cooperation. *News Central Asia* (blog). July 20. https://www.newscentralasia.net/2024/07/20/turkmenistan-kazakhstan-afghanistan-enhance-transport-cooperation/.

Nurmatov, Ernist. 2024. Kyrgyz-Uzbek border: How will the opening of checkpoints impact the economy? (in Russian). Radio Azattyk. September 13. https://rus.azattyk.org/a/33118562.html.

Observatory of Economic Complexity. n.d. Kazakhstan trade statistics. Observatory of economic complexity.

Omirgazy, Dana. 2024. Kazakhstan, Turkmenistan intend to enhance partnership. *The Astana Times*, May 28. https://astanatimes.com/2024/05/kazakhstan-turkmenistan-intend-to-enhance-partnership/.

Orient. 2022. Turkmenistan and Uzbekistan signed agreements for 451 million US dollars. Orient. July 14. https://orient.tm/en/post/38791/turkmenistan-and-uzbekistan-signed-agreements-451-million-us-dollars.

Ortcom.kz. 2019. As of today, about 150 vehicles are at the Karasu checkpoint [in Russian]. Ortcom.kz. April 5. https://ortcom.kz/ru/novosti/pochemu-obrazovalas-ochered-transportnyh-sredstv-na-kazahstansko-kyrgyzskoj-granice.

Ospanova, Rufiya. 2013. Kazakhstan, Turkmenistan Presidents open new railroad crossing. *The Astana Times*, May 15. https://astanatimes.com/2013/05/kazakhstan-turkmenistan-presidents-open-new-railroad-crossing/.

Pamir Inside. 2021. 'Two Months Without Fresh Fruits and Vegetables': How Ethnic Kyrgyz in Murghab are coping after border closures with Kyrgyzstan. Pamir Inside. August 4. https://pam irinside.org/%d0%b4%d0%b2%d0%b0-%d0%bc%d0%b5%d1%81%d1%8f%d1%86%d0% b0-%d0%b1%d0%b5%d0%b7-%d1%81%d0%b2%d0%b5%d0%b6%d0%b8%d1%85-%d1% 84%d1%80%d1%83%d0%ba%d1%82%d0%be%d0%b2-%d0%b8-%d0%be%d0%b2%d0% be%d1%89%d0%b5/.

Panorama. 1997. Relations between Almaty and Bishkek Have Been Formalized [in Russian]. *Panorama (Kazakhstan)*, November 16.

Pestriakova, Marina. 2014. Economic Tandem [in Russian]. *Vecher.Kz*, November 15. Retrieved via Integrum World Wide database.

Popova, Marina. 2024. With European funding, it is planned to connect Kyzylorda and Uchkuduk by railway [in Russian]. InBusiness.kz. June 19. https://inbusiness.kz/ru/last/za-schet-evropejsk ogo-finansirovaniya-planiruetsya-soedinit-kyzylordu-i-uchkuduk-zheleznoj-dorogoj.

Population Reference Bureau. 2023. Population Trends in Asia. *Population Reference Bureau* (blog). 2023. https://2023-wpds.prb.org/asia/.
President of the Republic of Kazakhstan. 1998. On the ratification of the treaty of eternal friendship between the Republic of Kazakhstan and the Kyrgyz Republic [in Kazakh]. https://adilet.zan.kz/kaz/docs/Z980000287_.
president.uz. 2023. The presidents expressed satisfaction with the fruitful outcomes of the visit. president.uz. January 1. https://president.uz/ru/lists/view/5846.
Putz, Catherine. 2024. Kazakhstan and Uzbekistan agree to install transboundary water meters. The Diplomat. March 20. https://thediplomat.com/2024/03/kazakhstan-and-uzbekistan-agree-to-install-transboundary-water-meters/.
QazIndustry. 2022. QazIndustry. May 23. https://qazindustry.gov.kz/zcbpjnhfkatebyt.html/article/2056-eksport-import-investitsii-proizvodstva-itogi-razvitiya-almatinskoy-oblasti-za-2020-god.
Radio Azattyk. 2022. The Kyrgyz and Uzbek foreign ministers signed a number of documents on border issues (in Kyrgyz). *Radio Azattyk*, November 3, sec. Жаңылыктар. https://www.azattyk.org/a/32113866.html.
Radio Azattyk. 2023. Kazakhstan and Russia Sign a Border Agreement: What Does It Mean? [in Russian]. January 27. https://rus.azattyq.org/a/32243536.html.
Radio Free Europe/Radio Liberty. 2020. Report: Tajik-Uzbek border cleared of mines. *Radio Free Europe/Radio Liberty*, January 6, sec. Uzbekistan. https://www.rferl.org/a/report-tajik-uzbek-border-cleared-of-mines/30362369.html.
Radio Ozodi. 2024a. The 'Kara-Suu' checkpoint, closed since 2010, has officially reopened on the Kyrgyz-Uzbek border (in Russian). Radio Ozodi. September 12. https://rus.ozodi.org/a/na-kyrgyzsko-uzbekskoy-granitse-otkrylsya-ne-rabotavshiy-s-2010-goda-punkt-propuska-kara-suu-/33117033.html.
Radio Ozodi. 2024b. Uzbekistan and Tajikistan discussed the demarcation of their shared border (in Russian). Радио Озоди. May 6. https://rus.ozodi.org/a/uzbekistan-i-tadzhikistan-obsudili-protsess-demarkatsii-obschey-granitsy/32934782.html.
Radio Ozodlik. 2017. The border between Uzbekistan and Turkmenistan was reopened ahead of Mirziyoyev's visit to Khorezm (in Russian). Radio Ozodlik. January 30. https://rus.ozodlik.org/a/28264939.html.
Radiosy Azatlyk. 2024. Increasing number of Turkmen traveling to Kazakhstan leads to more pressure on travelers from security services [in Turkmen]. Azatlyk Radiosy. February 14. https://www.azathabar.com/a/gazagystana-gidyan-turkmenlerin-kopelmegi-bilen-howpsuzlyk-gulluklarynyn-syyahatcylara-basyslary-artyar/32819314.html.
Rahmatov, Zhasur. 2024. Uzbekistan and Tajikistan: Advancing strategic partnership and alliance. Isrz.Uz. April 17. https://isrs.uz/ru/maqolalar/uzbekistan-i-tadzikistan-na-puti-k-ukrepleniu-strategiceskogo-partnerstva-i-souznicestva.
ReliefWeb. 2005. Kyrgyzstan-Tajikistan: Landmine threat along Uzbek border removed—Kyrgyzstan. October 31. https://reliefweb.int/report/kyrgyzstan/kyrgyzstan-tajikistan-landmine-threat-along-uzbek-border-removed.
Rickleton, Chris. 2023. 'The border of friendship': What do the agreements between Kyrgyzstan and Uzbekistan promise? (in Russian). *Radio Azattyq*, February 1, sec. Центральная Азия. https://rus.azattyq.org/a/32250519.html.
Rickleton, Chris. 2024. Farewell Barak: Uzbekistan absorbs Kyrgyz Exclave as part of historic border deal. *Radio Free Europe/Radio Liberty*, April 23, sec. Kyrgyzstan. https://www.rferl.org/a/uzbekistan-kyrgyzstan-barak-exclave-historic-border-deal/32917744.html.
Rosbach, Kristian. 2023. Maximizing the Potential of the Almaty-Bishkek Economic Corridor. Development Asia. February 9. https://development.asia/case-study/maximizing-potential-almaty-bishkek-economic-corridor.
Rosset, Damian, and David Svarin. 2014. The constraints of the past and the failure of Central Asian Regionalism, 1991–2004. *The Region* 3 (2): 245–266.

References

Skripnik, Galina. 2017. Customs checkpoints on the border between Kazakhstan and Kyrgyzstan to be modernized [in Russian]. Kazinform. April 24. https://www.inform.kz/ru/tamozhennye-punkty-na-granice-kazahstana-i-kyrgyzstana-moderniziruyut_a3020283.

Smekhova, Maiya. 2022. Funding for business: Uzbek-Kyrgyz Development Fund opens in Bishkek. Mir 24. April 14. https://mir24.tv/news/16504503/dengi-na-bizes-v-bishkeke-otkryl sya-uzbeksko-kyrgyzskii-fond-razvitiya.

Spot.uz. 2023. Uzkaztrade to import fruits and vegetables from Uzbekistan to Kazakhstan wholesale. Spot.uz. April 17. https://www.spot.uz/ru/2023/04/17/fruits-for-kz/.

Spot.uz. 2024a. Checkpoint capacity between Uzbekistan and Kazakhstan to Triple. spot.uz. March 4. https://www.spot.uz/ru/2024/03/04/customs-control/.

Spot.uz. 2024b. The Uzbek-Tajik investment company plans to implement 14 projects worth $135 million. Spot.uz. April 18. https://www.spot.uz/ru/2024/04/18/tajikistan-projects/.

Starkov, Aleksei. 2024. New road to Issyk-Kul: When will it be built and how much will it cost? [In Russian]. Kolesa.Kz. September 19. https://kolesa.kz/content/news/novaya-doroga-na-issyk-kul-kogda-postroyat-i-pochyom-budet-proezd/.

State Revenue Committee. 2023. Modernization of Tazhen and Temir Baba Border Checkpoints in Mangystau Region Underway [in Kazakh]. Government of Kazakhstan. May 11. https://www.gov.kz/memleket/entities/kgd/press/news/details/552427?lang=kk.

Statistics Agency Under the president of the Republic of Uzbekistan. 2024a. Demography. Stat.Uz. 2024. https://www.stat.uz/en/official-statistics/demography.

Statistics Agency Under the president of the Republic of Uzbekistan. 2024b. Foreign Economic Activity (in Russian). Stat.Uz. 2024. https://stat.uz/ru/ofitsialnaya-statistika/merchandise-trade.

Stepanova, Tamara, and Salamat Bekbaev. 2024. The area of the Ustyurt Reserve will increase by 640 thousand hectares [in Russian]. 24.kz. April 20. https://24.kz/ru/news/ekologiya/item/648 988-ploshchad-ustyurtskogo-zapovednika-uvelichitsya-na-640-tysyach-ga.

Sultan, Assel. 2018. Will Kazakhstan and Uzbekistan become competitors? [in Russian]. *CABAR.asia* (blog). April 9. https://cabar.asia/ru/stanut-li-kazakhstan-i-uzbekistan-konkur entami.

Sultanalieva, Syinat. 2022. Kyrgyzstan-Tajikistan border clashes prove deadly for Civilians. Hrw.org. September 21. https://www.hrw.org/news/2022/09/21/kyrgyzstan-tajikistan-border-clashes-prove-deadly-civilians.

Suyarkulova, Mohira. 2012. *Statehood as dialogue: Conflicting historical narratives of Tajikistan and Uzbekistan*. In The Transformation of Tajikistan: Routledge.

Time.kz. 2019. Kazakhstan and Turkmenistan intend to increase mutual trade volumes [in Russian]. Time.kz. March 12. https://time.kz/news/economics/2019/03/12/kazahstan-i-turkmenistan-nam erenny-narashhivat-obemy-vzaimnoj-torgovli.

Toguzbaev, Kazis. 2017. Turkmenistan: You can't drive from Kazakhstan, only fly. Azattyq. February 17. https://rus.azattyq.org/a/kazakhstan-turkmenistan-perevozki/28313855.html.

Tokaev, K.-Zh., and Z. Amanzholova. 2014. *The Truth about the State Border of the Republic of Kazakhstan* [in Russian]. Almaty: Zhibek Zholy.

Toktogulov, Beishenbek. 2022. Uzbekistan's Foreign Policy under Mirziyoyev: Change or continuity? *Eurasian Research Journal* 4 (1): 49–67. https://doi.org/10.53277/2519-2442-2022. 1-03.

Transparency International. 2024. 2023 corruption perceptions index: Explore the results. Transparency.Org. January 30. https://www.transparency.org/en/cpi/2023.

Treaty on Strategic Partnership Between the Republic of Kazakhstan and Turkmenistan [in Kazakh]. 2017. https://adilet.zan.kz/kaz/docs/Z1800000137.

Türkmen Döwlet Habarlary. 2024. Cooperation between Turkmenistan and Uzbekistan's Regions Is Being Strengthened [in Turkmen]. Türkmen Döwlet Habarlary. November 21. https://tdh.gov.tm/tk/post/43059/turkmenistanyn-we-ozbegistanyn-sebitlerinin-arasyndaky-hyzmatdas lyk-pugtalandyrylyar.

Tusupbekova, Laura. 2024. Investor needed to build hub on Kyrgyzstan Border. Kazpravda.Kz. May 16. https://kazpravda.kz/n/nuzhen-investor-dlya-stroitelstva-haba-na-granitse-s-kyrgyzstanom/.

UNDP. n.d.-a. Climate change and resilience in Central Asia. UNDP. https://www.undp.org/eurasia/projects/climate-change-and-resilience-central-asia. Accessed 2 Dec 2024.

UNDP. n.d.-b. Cross-border cooperation for sustainable peace and development. UNDP. https://www.undp.org/tajikistan/projects/cross-border-cooperation-sustainable-peace-and-development. Accessed 2 Dec 2024.

United Nations General Assembly. 2021. Resolution 75/278: Declaring the Aral Sea Region a zone of ecological innovations and technologies. United Nations. https://documents.un.org/doc/undoc/gen/n21/123/38/pdf/n2112338.pdf?OpenElement.

Vesti.kz. 2010. Kazakhstan will open its border with Kyrgyzstan for all goods [in Russian]. Vesti.kz. July 16. https://vesti.kz/kazahstan/kazahstan-otkroet-granitsu-s-kirgiziey-dlya-vseh-tovarov-57909/.

Vorotnoi, Igor. 2013. Leaders of Kazakhstan and Turkmenistan inaugurated the Uzen–Gorgan road section [in Russian]. *Izvestia Kazakhstan*, May 14.

World Bank. 2019. Uzbekistan: Toward a new, more open economy. World Bank. Summer 2019. https://www.worldbank.org/en/country/uzbekistan/publication/economic-update-summer-2019.

World Bank. 2021. Climate and Environment program in Central Asia. World Bank Group. June 9. https://www.worldbank.org/en/topic/environment/brief/climate-and-environment-program-in-central-asia.

World Bank. 2023. World Bank open data. 2023. https://data.worldbank.org.

World Bank. 2024. Tajikistan. World Bank Open Data. 2024. https://data.worldbank.org.

World Bank. n.d. Development projects: Third phase of the Central Asia Regional links program (CARs-3)—P159220. Text/HTML. World Bank. https://projects.worldbank.org/en/projects-operations/project-detail/P159220. Accessed 2 Dec 2024.

Yusupov, Yuliy. 2024. Foreign trade of Central Asian countries: Trends, barriers, and prospects. Part 1. CAPS Unlock. https://capsunlock.org/?page_id=41.

Zakon.kz. 2011. Challenges of crossing the Kazakhstan-Kyrgyzstan border [in Russian]. Zakon.kz. October 10. https://online.zakon.kz/Document/?doc_id=31064772.

Zhaik Press. 2024. Passenger trains will begin operating from Nukus to the resort region of Mangystau in Kazakhstan [in Russian]. Zhaik Press. August 2. https://zhaikpress.kz/ru/news/iz-nukusa-v-kurortnyj-region-kazaxstana-mangistau-nachnut-kursirovat-passazhirskie-poezda/.

Open Access This chapter is licensed under the terms of the Creative Commons Attribution 4.0 International License (http://creativecommons.org/licenses/by/4.0/), which permits use, sharing, adaptation, distribution and reproduction in any medium or format, as long as you give appropriate credit to the original author(s) and the source, provide a link to the Creative Commons license and indicate if changes were made.

The images or other third party material in this chapter are included in the chapter's Creative Commons license, unless indicated otherwise in a credit line to the material. If material is not included in the chapter's Creative Commons license and your intended use is not permitted by statutory regulation or exceeds the permitted use, you will need to obtain permission directly from the copyright holder.

Chapter 4
Adapting Global Cross-Border Cooperation Experiences for Central Asia

To analyze the applicability of international CBC practices to the realities of Central Asia, we will attempt, based on the analysis conducted in the relevant chapter and without claiming exhaustive coverage of the issue, to outline the typical features of such cooperation and assess their relevance to the models of various regions from a comparative perspective. The results are summarized in the Table 4.1.

The most universal feature of CBC across various regions is the support for cross-border infrastructure development projects, primarily funded through national budgets. Another relatively common practice is the use of CBC to promote the development of border regions. However, this approach requires significant financial commitments from central governments combined with a willingness to grant these regions a degree of autonomy for cross-border cooperation. A widely used model, particularly in Asia, involves the creation of cross-border economic cooperation zones with diverse specializations, such as trade, logistics, manufacturing, and others. Some countries and regions have achieved considerable success in attracting external donor funding for the implementation of CBC projects. Some countries and regions are making efforts to support and formalize informal cross-border trade, although these initiatives have so far yielded mixed results in most cases.

Certain aspects of national or regional CBC experiences are particularly specific. For instance, the EU's initiative to establish cross-border regions with autonomous formal powers in certain areas has not been fully replicated outside the EU, although informal cross-border regionalism can be found in North America. Notable aspects of North American cooperation include effective project-oriented activism and the establishment of systematic dialogue between official and unofficial actors on border management issues. China has managed to combine a rigid top-down governance approach with flexibility in granting certain regions autonomy for implementing CBC initiatives. The ASEAN model of growth triangles, while original yet bearing some similarities to the EU's cross-border meso-regionalism, represents one more distinctive approach that has been sporadically attempted in other regions.

Table 4.1 Typical features of CBC in selected countries and regions

Region/CBC feature	EU	North America	China	ASEAN	Latin America	Africa	Russia
Effective cross-border regions	v	o					
Wide formal CBC powers of local authorities	v						
Competitive funding for CBC projects	v					o	
Cross-border infrastructure development	v	v	v	o	v		o
Building cross-border mesoregions	v			v			
Empowering selected borderland regions by a central government			v				
CBC as a tool for development of borderland regions	v		v		o		
Border economic zones			v	v	o		o
Project-oriented bottom-up CBC	o	v					
Institutionalized dialogue between official and non-governmental actors on border crossing management		v					
Extensive engagement of third-party funding for CBC projects			o	o	v		

(continued)

4 Adapting Global Cross-Border Cooperation Experiences for Central Asia

Table 4.1 (continued)

Region/CBC feature	EU	North America	China	ASEAN	Latin America	Africa	Russia
Top-down cross-border regionalism as a tool for implementing governmental foreign policy strategies			v				v
Application of foreign experiences to national or regional CBC strategies				o	v	v	o
CBC as a tool for ethnic conflict management	v						
Support for cross-border informal trade			o	o			

v—high degree of phenomenon prevalence
o—moderate degree of phenomenon prevalence

The adoption of external CBC models and experiences remains limited in scale. Elements of the EU's experience in CBC have been evident in Africa and Latin America and were also applied in Russia before 2022. Similarly, the spread of China's experience with border economic zones is evident, as such zones have been established in Southeast Asia, Russia, and Latin America. Attempts to implement the growth triangle model outside ASEAN have been inconsistent and not particularly successful. At the same time, the CBC experiences of Latin America, Africa, and even the relatively successful North American model remain underutilized. Yet, these regions have significant innovative achievements, and even the shortcomings of their experiences provide valuable lessons for developing more effective CBC policies.

When assessing the applicability of international CBC practices to Central Asian realities, identifying the key limitations is crucial. These limitations primarily include the authoritarian and centralized nature of governance in Central Asian regimes, the limited financial resources available for funding CBC initiatives, and the high levels of corruption in the region.

Centralized authoritarian political regimes in the region pose a significant obstacle to replicating European-style cross-border regionalism, which relies on granting extensive powers to regions and legally empowering cross-border region-building. Moreover, the authoritarian somewhat unfavorable conditions for North American-style project-oriented cooperation, which is largely rooted in private initiative and activism. In both cases, the core issue lies in the likelihood that centralized authoritarian regimes would view any weakening of their control over their administrative regions or the growth of cross-border social activism with suspicion.

This challenge is particularly pronounced in Turkmenistan, the most closed country in the region, which strictly limits uncontrolled interactions with the outside world.

Nevertheless, it cannot be ruled out that regionalism and project-oriented activism, adapted to Central Asian conditions, could prove viable. Such adaptation might involve, for instance, liberalizing opportunities for cross-border activities carried out by networks and other institutions with a technocratic focus, aimed at addressing priority areas for the region and border territories, such as water conservation, renewable energy adoption, and sustainable agriculture. To encourage cross-border cooperation in these or other areas, Central Asian authorities could draw on the European experience of granting legal personality to cross-border organizations or the North American experience of fostering project-oriented interregional partnerships. Examples include cross-border regions like Cascadia or the less ambitious CaliBaja project, in which the neighboring side holds only an advisory role in initiatives predominantly led by one of the parties.

The second limitation lies in the scarcity of funding available for the development of CBC in Central Asia. This issue is particularly pronounced in Kyrgyzstan and Tajikistan. Such financial constraints primarily hinder the full-scale replication of the EU's Interreg program, large-scale cross-border infrastructure planning, and the implementation of ambitious border region development programs inspired by the Chinese model, or the development of cross-border infrastructure following the North American example.

Some options for mobilizing funding on a smaller scale still exist. For example, the experience of ECOWAS—both its successes and failures—provides a useful reference, as it effectively attempts to implement a locally adapted equivalent of the Interreg program with significantly more modest funding. Another option could involve more active engagement of external support to implement CBC projects, drawing on the experiences of African and Southeast Asian countries, as well as Latin America in the context of establishing transboundary protected areas. Currently, external donors have focused most of their efforts on the Fergana Valley, and it would be advisable for regional countries to encourage an expansion of this geographic scope. Among other possibilities, the Central Asian states, with the involvement of Afghanistan, could seek to replicate a locally adapted version of the Greater Mekong Subregion format in the Amu Darya basin. This project, largely implemented by countries with authoritarian political regimes and backed by substantial international financial support, offers a potentially relevant example.

The third significant limitation to applying international CBC practices in the region is the high level of corruption in Central Asian countries. Corruption can severely undermine the effectiveness of competitive funding projects modeled on Interreg, as well as programs for cross-border planning and regional development. Additionally, corruption has the potential to deter investors and foreign donors from committing to large-scale CBC projects.

To mitigate the impact of corruption on the development of CBC in Central Asia, it is essential to prioritize transparency and accountability mechanisms for the allocation and use of funds. In certain cases, such as implementing competitive funding programs for CBC projects modeled on Interreg, involving external experts from outside the region in overseeing such financing should be considered. Additionally, conducting studies and sharing experiences with international consultants on anti-corruption measures in CBC project implementation would be highly advisable.

Beyond these limitations, Central Asian countries have broader opportunities to draw on international CBC practices. Some aspects of this experience, such as the establishment of border economic zones, are already being actively implemented in the region. Additionally, other elements of international experience merit attention, including the creation of cross-border mesoregions modeled on European or Southeast Asian examples, the use of top-down cross-border regionalism as a tool for advancing Central Asian integration informed by Russian experience, empowering selected borderland regions by central governments following the Chinese model, encouraging intensive institutionalized dialogue between official and non-governmental actors on border crossing management in line with the North American approach, employing CBC as a tool for managing ethnic conflicts based on EU practices, and supporting informal cross-border trade while taking into account the successes and challenges of Chinese, Southeast Asian, and African experiences. It should be noted that the recommendations presented below are not ready-made practical solutions but rather potential strategic directions whose applicability to Central Asian conditions requires further detailed assessment.

Building mesoregions could become a tool for enhancing CBC by leveraging more substantial potentials than those of administrative regions directly adjacent to the border. Additionally, promoting cross-border meso-regionalism might seem less problematic to Central Asian authorities than encouraging cross-border regions composed of two provinces from neighboring countries. This is because the risk of mesoregions falling out of central government control is lower, given the difficulty of aligning interests among a larger number of actors.

European-style meso-regionalism, which primarily involves significantly expanding the number of cooperating regions to include those not directly adjacent to the border, could be utilized to foster cross-border cooperation in desert or mountainous areas with poor transport proximity. For instance, it could be considered to enhance cooperation among desert regions in Kazakhstan, Uzbekistan, and potentially Turkmenistan, where the development of CBC between neighboring regions is hindered by the scarcity of cross-border transport links and the vast distances between settlements in neighboring countries. In such cases, broadening the range of participating regions could expand the scope of cooperation, the pool of partners, and the logistical opportunities by utilizing the transport and other infrastructures of a greater number of participants.

Southeast Asian-style meso-regionalism, specifically the creation of growth triangles (or "growth polygons"), could provide a more systematic approach to the combined utilization of complementary potentials among participating parties.

Despite the sharp asymmetry in economic capacities between Kazakhstan and Uzbekistan on one side and Kyrgyzstan and Tajikistan on the other, the latter also possess unique advantages in water resources, energy, and (in the case of Kyrgyzstan) tourism. These advantages enable them to make valuable and distinct contributions to the formation of mutually complementary growth triangles.

Top-down cross-border regionalism, controlled by central authorities and primarily limited to interregional cooperation forums, despite its constraints, can still play a role in intensifying cross-border interactions in Central Asia. This approach could contribute to enhancing the effectiveness of economic cooperation among Central Asian countries, fostering stronger social and cultural ties, and ultimately advancing regional integration. To maximize the potential of this tool, it would be useful to examine the experiences of countries that utilize it, such as Russia, which promotes it in the context of Eurasian Economic Union integration. Notably, as of late 2024, 20 interregional cooperation forums had been held between Russia and Kazakhstan and 11 between Russia and Belarus, significantly exceeding the number of similar forums conducted among Central Asian countries. However, when analyzing Russia's experience with top-down cross-border regionalism, it is important to consider its vulnerabilities. Efforts should focus on making such forums less bureaucratic, more results-oriented, and less dominated by the most powerful participants whenever possible.

Empowering selected borderland regions by a central government, following the Chinese model, could involve encouraging provincial initiatives for developing CBC in a limited range of areas. These areas would not entail the creation of cross-border regional institutions with broad autonomy but rather focus on activities such as facilitating cross-border trade, fostering industrial cooperation, and developing infrastructure. Such initiatives could strategically utilize CBC as a tool for advancing those borderland regions capable of presenting viable development proposals, for instance, by improving the logistical, trade, and industrial potential through strengthened cross-border ties. Empowered regions could receive prioritized financial support from the central government within agreed-upon limits, as well as benefit from privileged communication channels with central authorities. However, implementing such a model poses significant corruption risks, which must be properly addressed.

The systematic involvement of border regions, business entities, public representatives, and research centers in dialogue on optimizing border crossing procedures, characteristic of the North American experience, could yield significant economic benefits. These include reducing border delays, stimulating cross-border business activity, intensifying cross-border mobility, and minimizing high-profile incidents related to delays that occasionally strain relations between neighboring countries. In the context of Central Asia, such structures should be positioned as depoliticized and technocratic. At the same time, care must be taken to ensure that they do not become mere extensions of government bodies dominated by bureaucrats.

In the event of serious conflicts along Central Asian borders, such as the ongoing situation in the Isfara Valley on the border between Tajikistan and Kyrgyzstan, it would be worth considering to draw on the EU's experience in using CBC for conflict management. This approach is based on a consociational model, which involves a measured promotion of cross-border interactions. It begins with contacts in neutral areas where the interests of the parties are most aligned and gradually expands the scope of such engagements.

As noted earlier, one of the distinctive features of the situation in Central Asia, compared to the conditions fostering CBC in Europe or North America, is the prominent role of informal cross-border trade and border markets. While Western approaches do not offer relevant recipes for managing this issue, the experiences of China, Southeast Asia, and East Africa, with their respective successes and shortcomings, may be more applicable. Although these experiences are unlikely to provide clear success stories or ready-made solutions, further study of them could prove valuable in developing a region-specific Central Asian model for addressing this issue.

This study primarily focuses on the strategic aspects of CBC, paying considerably less attention to more specific recommendations for improvements at the micro level. Among the most commonly proposed recommendations for CBC in the Central Asian region are the aforementioned controlled support for the informal cross-border economy (primarily trade) and the regulation of borderland market operations, the modernization of cross-border transport infrastructure, and the facilitation of cross-border mobility. Another key measure is fostering dialogue between local communities on the allocation of water and land resources.

A substantial number of specific recommendations for developing local CBC in the Fergana Valley were proposed in the aforementioned report by the CAREC Institute. In addition to the previously mentioned suggestions, the report emphasizes the development of cross-border production aimed at creating value chains through the use of advanced technologies, facilitating border business access to affordable credit, improving the skills of producers and other entrepreneurs, and empowering local organizations (such as water user associations, pasture user groups, farmers, and women's organizations). Further recommendations include improving access to information about cross-border business and employment opportunities, developing a complementary healthcare system and cross-border services in this area, supporting the organization of cross-border business forums, and encouraging cooperation in tourism, culture, and education (Asian Development Bank 2020).

It should also be noted that the effective and systematic use of CBC practices from other regions is not yet a strong point for Central Asian states or the vast majority of other countries. The systematization and adaptation of such experiences could prove beneficial not only for Central Asia but also for other regions and countries around the world.

Reference

Asian Development Bank. 2020. *Strengthening Cross-Border Community Collaboration in the CAREC Region: A Scoping Study*, 0 ed. Manila, Philippines: Asian Development Bank. https://doi.org/10.22617/TCS200414-2.

Open Access This chapter is licensed under the terms of the Creative Commons Attribution 4.0 International License (http://creativecommons.org/licenses/by/4.0/), which permits use, sharing, adaptation, distribution and reproduction in any medium or format, as long as you give appropriate credit to the original author(s) and the source, provide a link to the Creative Commons license and indicate if changes were made.

The images or other third party material in this chapter are included in the chapter's Creative Commons license, unless indicated otherwise in a credit line to the material. If material is not included in the chapter's Creative Commons license and your intended use is not permitted by statutory regulation or exceeds the permitted use, you will need to obtain permission directly from the copyright holder.

Conclusion

International experience with CBC encompasses a wide range of starting conditions, priorities, strategies, and practices. While the European Union's CBC is often considered the most advanced and successful, the conditions that shaped this experience—such as open internal borders, integration of CBC into broader regional development and integration priorities, substantial funding, and significant regional autonomy to foster cross-border ties—are unusual on a global scale and can be seen as more of an exception than the rule. In contrast, the conditions under which Central Asian CBC evolves—characterized by authoritarian regimes, centralized governance, and limited funding—are not exceptional but fairly typical in a global context. This does not, however, present an insurmountable obstacle to applying lessons from the EU or other regions that deviate from the global norm. Rather than wholesale replication, the focus should be on selecting and adapting elements of these experiences to align with local circumstances.

When considering the applicability of international experience to the realities of Central Asia, it is important to take into account not only the strengths but also the problematic aspects of such experience.

The EU's CBC experience can be seen as a sophisticated toolkit that includes instruments such as cross-border regionalism, multilevel governance, competitive funding programs for cross-border projects, legal mechanisms for establishing transboundary legal entities, and the use of consociational CBC to address ethnopolitical conflicts, among others. These tools, combined with the transparency of internal EU borders, enable European CBC to thrive across a variety of domains. However, not all of these instruments function effectively even within the EU itself, let alone in its external CBC efforts (e.g., between the EU and its neighbors). Persistent challenges remain, such as insufficient incentives for active cooperation, instable cross-border networks, and enduring cultural barriers.

CBC in other regions, compared to Europe, is marked by a more economical approach both in terms of the funding allocated for its development and the range of areas in which it evolves.

North American CBC has generally been effective in reducing border control barriers and mobilizing cross-border activism to address environmental issues.

However, challenges such as limited funding and the shifting political climate in the United States raise questions about its stability, while a lack of mutual trust diminishes its effectiveness along the U.S.–Mexico border.

The Chinese model is characterized by flexibility in balancing a centralized authoritarian political system with granting decision-making autonomy to border regions. Additionally, border-adjacent economic zones have proven to be a versatile and, in many cases, effective framework for facilitating interactions, accommodating both informal traders and officially registered businesses of various sizes. However, the challenges of the Chinese model include its unilateral approach, with insufficient adaptation to the contexts of its partners, as well as a lack of accountability, which can result in inefficient resource allocation.

For ASEAN member states, characterized by political diversity and the predominance of centralized governance systems, CBC is generally not a key political priority, and its outcomes are relatively modest. At the same time, ASEAN's meso-regionalism, exemplified by the development of growth triangles based on the pooling of complementary resources among participants, has proven to be a relatively effective model. Despite coordination challenges, this approach has achieved notable success, including its limited adoption beyond the ASEAN region. Particular attention should be given to the Greater Mekong Subregion model, which, despite its limited effectiveness and vague governance mechanisms, has managed to sustain interactions among diverse actors, including authoritarian states with centralized governance, Chinese regions, and major international donors.

The experience of Latin America, where CBC demonstrates mixed results, is valuable not only for its significant achievements but also for the lessons that can be drawn from the serious challenges limiting its effectiveness—even in seemingly favorable conditions of cultural and linguistic proximity between the cooperating countries' territories. On the one hand, states in the region strive to involve regional authorities and non-state actors in CBC, fund large-scale development projects for border areas and cross-border connectivity, prioritize CBC within their integration agendas, and attract foreign funding to systematically support transboundary environmental projects. On the other hand, the effectiveness of such cooperation is significantly undermined by strict centralized control over cross-border projects and, especially, by severe political disagreements that periodically arise between the cooperating countries.

The diverse experiences of CBC in Africa often unfold under challenging conditions, including artificial borders that are poorly defined and weakly controlled by governments, poverty, limited financial resources of governments, political instability, and weak cross-border transport infrastructure. Nevertheless, African CBC has achieved noteworthy successes in some cases, such as integrating CBC into regional integration agendas, implementing competitive funding programs, effectively securing external funding, managing some borders jointly, and supporting informal cross-border trade.

The experience of Russian CBC can be considered even more contentious, as its effectiveness is hindered by centralized bureaucratic control. At the same time, this experience offers valuable lessons of both a positive and negative nature, including the mixed success of Russia's attempts to adapt elements of European and Chinese CBC models to its own context, as well as the use of top-down regionalism as a tool for Russia-dominated Eurasian integration.

The specificity of Central Asian CBC is largely shaped by a combination of political, social, and economic conditions in the region. Politically, the region is dominated by authoritarian regimes with centralized governance, which significantly limits the autonomy of border regions in establishing cross-border connections. Nevertheless, Uzbekistan's recent efforts to revitalize CBC along its borders with all Central Asian states demonstrate that a top-down approach can also serve as a catalyst for cooperation.

Economically, the landlocked position of Central Asian countries plays a crucial role, driving efforts to develop regional cross-border transport networks and border logistics hubs. However, for most countries in the region, economic cooperation with one another is not a top priority, as they tend to favor more attractive extra-regional economic partners. The financial capacity of Central Asian states to support CBC remains limited. Socially, unlike the EU, Central Asia experiences population growth in border areas, which creates challenges for ensuring employment. Additionally, informal cross-border trade and border markets play a particularly significant role.

A pressing issue for border areas is the need to address the growing scarcity of water and land resources, which is, in some cases, critical for preventing the escalation of transboundary ethnopolitical conflicts. In this regard, the ability of Tajikistan and Kyrgyzstan to restore their currently halted cross-border ties will serve as an important test. Recent border negotiations and the easing of post-conflict tensions offer a glimmer of hope for progress.

It is important to recognize that the Central Asian region is far from homogeneous, with each country possessing its own unique characteristics. Geographically, cooperation with neighboring countries within the region is most crucial for Uzbekistan, a double-landlocked country that shares borders exclusively with other Central Asian states and Afghanistan. Economically, Kazakhstan and Uzbekistan have the greatest potential for such cooperation, including the ability to finance joint cross-border projects. These two countries are better positioned than others in the region to act as policymakers, while Kyrgyzstan and Tajikistan, with more limited resources, are more likely to take on the role of policy-takers. At the same time, Kyrgyzstan has developed the region's most liberal political system, which provides actors with greater autonomy to implement cross-border projects, whereas Turkmenistan has the least liberal system, strictly restricting cross-border interactions.

The potential for adapting external models to Central Asian realities should be assessed through the lens of several constraints: the authoritarian and centralized nature of local governance systems, limited financial resources, and high levels of corruption. These constraints complicate the implementation of models based on cross-border regionalism, decision-making autonomy for border regions, cross-border activism, and large-scale funding of cross-border projects without robust accountability mechanisms. Nevertheless, these limitations do not fundamentally preclude the adoption of an adapted top-down regionalism model, with limited regional autonomy for addressing a clearly defined set of issues, the encouragement of manageable cross-border activism, or the implementation of Interreg-style projects on a smaller scale with well-developed accountability mechanisms.

Beyond these constraints, Central Asia has access to an even broader arsenal of CBC strategies. These could include cross-border development planning for adjacent territories, the establishment of transboundary mesoregions modeled on European or ASEAN examples, the empowerment of selected border regions by central governments, institutionalized dialogue involving both governmental and non-governmental actors on managing cross-border flows, and more systematic efforts to create border economic zones, support informal cross-border trade, and attract external donors to fund CBC projects. Additionally, a consociational CBC model could be employed for conflict management purposes.

This list is far from exhaustive, particularly given that this work is primarily focused on strategies rather than more specific techniques for organizing CBC. We hope that this study serves as a useful step toward more detailed and thorough examination of the specifics of CBC in individual regions (especially beyond the EU and North America), as well as the development of new comparative cross-regional studies on CBC and, finally, well-grounded conceptualizations of CBC in a global perspective. These conceptualizations should be free from the currently dominant Eurocentric bias while creatively evaluating the potential applicability of European experiences beyond their original context. While this work is centered on assessing the potential for adapting international experiences to the specific conditions of post-Soviet Central Asia, we also hope that the monograph will draw the attention of researchers and practitioners to more systematic studies of the applicability of global CBC practices to the specific contexts of other regions. The effective use of such experiences could contribute to improving the living conditions of vast populations in border areas worldwide and fostering better relations between communities in adjacent territories of neighboring countries.

Bibliography

Agbiboa, Daniel E. 2017. Borders that continue to bother us: The politics of cross-border security cooperation in Africa's Lake Chad Basin. *Commonwealth & Comparative Politics* 55 (4): 403–425. https://doi.org/10.1080/14662043.2017.1312730.

Akorda. 2024. The President of Kazakhstan held extended talks with the President of Turkmenistan [in Kazakh]. *Akorda.kz*. October 10. https://www.akorda.kz/kz/memleket-basshysy-turikmens tan-prezidentimen-keneytilgen-kuramda-kelissoz-zhurgizdi-109126.

Allison, Roy. 2008. Virtual regionalism, regional structures and regime security in Central Asia. *Central Asian Survey* 27 (2): 185–202. https://doi.org/10.1080/02634930802355121.

Bohr, Annette. 2004. Regionalism in Central Asia: New geopolitics, old regional order. *International Affairs (Royal Institute of International Affairs 1944-)* 80 (3): 485–502.

Coronado, Irasema. 2014. Whither the Environmental nongovernmental organizations on multiple regions of the US–Mexico Border? *Journal of Borderlands Studies* 29 (4): 449–464. https://doi.org/10.1080/08865655.2014.982467.

Dobler, Gregor. 2016. The green, the grey and the blue: A typology of cross-border trade in Africa. *The Journal of Modern African Studies* 54 (1): 145–169. https://doi.org/10.1017/S0022278X 15000993.

Full Text: Vision and Actions on Jointly Building Belt and Road - Belt and Road Forum for International Cooperation. 2017. April 10. http://2017.beltandroadforum.org/english/n100/2017/0410/c22-45.html.

Internet Portal of the Commonwealth of Independent States. 2024. How Uzbekistan's Foreign trade changed in 2023 [in Russian]. Internet Portal of the Commonwealth of Independent States. January 26. https://e-cis.info/news/566/115397/.

Krapohl, Sebastian, and Alexandra Vasileva-Dienes. 2020. The region that isn't: China, Russia and the failure of regional integration in Central Asia. *Asia Europe Journal* 18 (3): 347–366. https://doi.org/10.1007/s10308-019-00548-0.

Ministry of Foreign Affairs of the Republic of Tajikistan. 2013. Territorial and border-related issues | Ministry of Foreign Affairs of the Republic of Tajikistan. Ministry of Foreign Affairs of the Republic of Tajikistan. March 1. https://mfa.tj/en/main/foreign-policy/territorial-and-border-iss ues?utm_source=chatgpt.com.

The Belfast Agreement. n.d. GOV.UK. https://www.gov.uk/government/publications/the-belfast-agreement. Accessed 14 Nov 2024.

View Treaty—Canada.Ca. n.d. https://www.treaty-accord.gc.ca/text-texte.aspx?id=105453. Accessed 20 Nov 2024.

Walther, Olivier. 2009. A mobile idea of space. traders, patrons and the cross-border economy in Sahelian Africa. *Journal of Borderlands Studies* 24 (1): 34–46. https://doi.org/10.1080/088 65655.2009.9695716.

The manufacturer's authorised representative in the EU is Springer Nature Customer Service Centre GmbH, Europaplatz 3, 69115 Heidelberg, Germany. If you have any concerns regarding our products, please contact ProductSafety@springernature.com

Printed and bound by CPI Group (UK) Ltd, Croydon, CR0 4YY

23/03/2026

02076360-0014